AUTHOR'S NOTE

It is considered a cliché to reiterate that truth is stranger than fiction. This book is not a cliché.

In the pages that follow you will discover the poignant happenings, the unusual people and the just plain weird things that happened to a real flesh and blood person. I wasn't looking to live on the edge—the "edgy" and novel and outrageous found me.

Perhaps your reaction will be like the young woman who, at a church singles group I spoke with, noted that I had too much experience for her to imagine me as a minister. If you like your understanding of the spiritual life to be black and white, cut and dried, this book may either leave you shaking your head or wondering where I am "coming from."

If you have, however, an understanding that the spiritual life is a narrow way that is high and lifted up, like a tightrope, you might hold your breath as I try to keep my balance and find my way guided only by the Spirit, my conscience and intuition.

My goal is to leave you laughing, crying, smiling, chuckling and nodding your head in the realization that you have met some of the same kind of people as I have in my years in the ministry. The church power broker, the suffering addict, the innocent struggling to understand the hard realities of life, the broken and misplaced, the "party girls," the manipulators of a kid's game into life and death and those who have had the spark of life beaten out of them.

This book represents the journey of a lifetime of serving others. The true events described are widely separated in time. Names and details have been changed to protect the innocent and the guilty. I hope you enjoy the trip.

Keith A. Rasey
Medina, Ohio

TABLE OF CONTENTS

Chapter One

POLAR BEAR ANGELS

Elinda's mother was not a member of the church I served as pastor. She did live in the neighborhood of the church in a section of New Haven known as Fairborn. A couple I was working with on premarital counseling had told her about my ability to listen well and draw together disparate thoughts into sensible insights.

I had no idea why she was coming to see me because all she had shared on the phone was a desire to talk with me about a problem their family was having. The day of the appointment we introduced ourselves and she asked me to call her by her first name, Paula. She was dark haired, about thirty-five years of age, I guessed, but with the worry lines of an older woman. There were no laugh lines or even smile creases on her face From the smell of stale smoke, it was painfully obvious Paula was a chain smoker so I scanned the office to be sure the ashtray was handy for her.

The introductory class on pastoral counseling I was taking had taught me enough to realize it was important to practice graciousness and hospitality to put her at ease, especially, as in this instance, when she was coming to talk with a stranger about something troubling. This was years before there was any concern about second hand smoke.

"So," I said in my best nondirective, Rogerian counseling voice, "you are hoping to talk with me to bring greater insight into a family member's underlying motivations?" It sure sounded good at the moment.

"Not exactly, "she responded. There was a long silence. I was being taught to let the silence hang around like an old friend.

"My daughter, Elinda is worrying me. She has started to really resist going to school in the morning. She is more moody than she has ever been and breaks out in tears if we mildly punish her."

"It's your daughter who is your concern, " I responded in my gentlest, nondirective voice. I waited for her response but there was none. Silence was failing me. "You're worried about her recent change in behavior—the school resistance and the moodiness."

That did bring a verbal response from her. We went through the family history covering such things as how long they had been married, how many children they had and their ages, job and location stability, birth order, etc. Nothing brought up any obvious precipitating event that might have triggered five-year old Elinda's behavior.

Elinda was the youngest of three children, her two older siblings being a boy of nine and a sister of fourteen. They were the third generation of their family to be born in America. Their family had lived in the same house for the past twelve years. The father had had the same blue collar job with the city for all of his adult life. Paula did not work outside the home.

Five-year old Elinda attended the same kindergarten in the same neighborhood elementary school that her siblings did or had. She had her own room and it had been her room for all of her life. Elinda had no more or less privileges than the other children of the family when they were the same age. None of her playmates had moved nor were there any new ones that had recently come over to play.

The hour was coming to a close. I gave Paula my card and shared that I would reflect and pray about what we had discussed. Perhaps that would make some connecting thread available to help us understand Elinda's behavior. We agreed to meet the next week.

In my naiveté I hoped that Elinda's mother and whole family would show up for worship the next Sunday. After all, it was the church that made it possible for me to be available to people in the neighborhood. It wasn't cheap maintaining a large, Italianate church building over one hundred years old. Nor was it inexpensive to have even a part-time, student minister around.

The salary, in 1977, was only $3000 per year, but the parsonage was a beautiful Queen Anne Victorian manse with ten foot ceilings and marble mirrors built into the walls. Although the house was past its prime, its granite fireplace and pure wool carpet—supposedly from the bar of a paddleboat steamer (this in a parsonage of a denomination historically part of the temperance movement)—gave it a dilapidated charm. But it was poorly insulated and almost required someone skilled in architectural restoration to maintain it.

That following Sunday morning, before the processional, I scanned the congregation hoping to see Paula and meet her daughter, Elinda. Knowing something about her from personal observation would have been helpful. But they were not in attendance, nor would they be in the future, as it turned out.

There was, however, a new woman, well-dressed, in the second to last pew on the lectern side of the sanctuary. It was my custom to walk down the center aisle of the church, ten or fifteen minutes before the service, to say hello to people and just be visible. This lady must have slipped in after I had gone back to warm up with the choir. No one claimed to know who she was so I went over and introduced myself to welcome her.

"You're just like all the rest!" she immediately cried out. "All you want to do is take my daughter away from me and take advantage of her."

"Ma'am," I stammered," I have never met you before today and know nothing of your daughter…." She interrupted me with an even louder voice.

"Yes, well you're just like all the other do-gooders who say they want to help but only want to take away things!!" She slammed her hymnal down on the floor, wrapped her expensive, fur lined coat around her shoulders and stormed out in righteous indignation.

I must have looked pretty shaken by this. Harold Barker, the Lay Leader, came over to reassure me. "She walks around the neighborhood talking to telephone poles and trees. Don't let it get to you."

The rest of the worship service went fine. Still, the naïve part of me that expected people to be grateful to God and to the church for helping them was bewildered by the responses of the stranger before worship and disappointed by the nonattendance of Elinda's family. Perhaps the

Buddhists are on to something when they say that one, who expects nothing, has all things.

Paula did show up promptly for our next counseling appointment. We made small talk and I tried to put her at ease by offering coffee. I confided, sheepishly, since I was supposedly the "expert" (what hubris!), that nothing had come to me about her daughter's behavior. I was careful to avoid the concern that occurred to me about her behavior being a response to some kind of violation of boundaries, as in molestation, for example.

As usual, it was the "client" herself who had the cause for the troubles besetting Elinda and affecting her family. Paula shared that the only thing that had come to her was the recent death of Elinda's eponymous paternal grandmother. I mentally kicked myself for not asking for more information on the extended family.

It wasn't just the death itself that was the issue. More pertinent was the fact that little Elinda was not allowed to attend the calling hours or the funeral service for the grandmother for whom she was named. She had put up quite a fuss about having to stay home with a babysitter while all of the other family members went. Elinda had thrown her favorite doll down the steps the day of the service and refused to eat any of the food sent over by the neighbors or friends of the family.

Paula explained that she had been encouraged by her family not to send Elinda to even the calling hours. Their feeling was that she was too young and that seeing her grandmother, Elinda in the coffin, would be too much for her to handle.

"I did the right thing as far as I knew, but now it looks like it wasn't the best for Elinda." Paula had started to cry.

"You acted on the best information you had and it hurts to feel it might not have been the best for Elinda?"

She nodded her head. There was a long silence before she continued, "I just don't know what to do to help her."

Thirty years afterwards, my experience tells me I was in over my head. What was probably the most helpful thing to do was to refer her to a child psychologist or a certified pastoral counselor for help in assisting her daughter through the maze of unexpressed grief, anger, resentment and depression. But I didn't know any better so I began to listen to my own emotions and my own "inner voice."

"I wonder how Elinda would feel about coming to see me to talk about how she feels now that Grandma is gone?" I waited for some response. Paula just picked up her head and looked me straight in the eye as if she were waiting for me to continue my thought. So, I did.

"Elinda could bring over some of her favorite things that Grandma gave her and tell me about them. Perhaps we could even play with them together or she could draw me a picture of Grandma in her new place."

At that last phrase, Paula looked a little unsure of the meaning.

"A drawing of how she sees Grandma now in her new home with God," I added. "Then we could ask Elinda, indirectly through play, what kind of ways she would like help with her grief." I didn't have a clue if a five year old would have such information but it was at least understandable to an adult.

Paula agreed. We set an appointment for me to meet alone with little Elinda the next Tuesday at 4 p.m. Today, with pastoral malpractice insurance and litigation paranoia—justified—about being alone behind a closed door with a member of the opposite sex or a child, I wonder if I would take the same kind of risk. Even with videotaping the entire interaction—with written parental permission—one must be careful to protect all concerned.

In the days before the appointment with little Elinda I was too busy to do much research on how to counsel children. Schoolwork was very time consuming and I had to keep the parish going at least enough to justify the congregation's expenditures on my salary and heating and maintaining a decaying manse. Every night my head hit the pillow with my energies too depleted to do anything but pray for little Elinda and ask for help in interacting with her in a way that was healing.

Crayons, at least, would not be hard to find as my own daughter, Michelle, was only four years of age and her mother, Marilyn, was running a home based childcare business from the parsonage. I rounded up several pieces of blank white paper and checked the supply of Hi-C to be sure I had something hospitable to offer Elinda.

Promptly on the appointed day, the doorbell rang and I met Elinda at last. The little five year old was a slender girl dressed in a Winnie-the-Pooh shift. She was carrying a small patent leather black purse exactly the right size for a little lady of her stature. Her hair was brown, medium length and her eyes green. Elinda had the look of a person more curious than scared and was trying hard to act older than her five years.

"Your mother has told me that you have had a hard time with your feelings since your Grandmother, Elinda, died. " She nodded. "Would you like to tell me about your Grandmother?"

Elinda was, at that very moment, taking a sip from her drinking glass. With most of her face swallowed up by the glass, she looked into my eyes as if she were trying to divine for herself if I really was going to listen to her feelings and cared about them. It was a little unnerving to be so frankly assessed by such a young child but I willed myself to keep the same kind, relaxed expression on my face as she read my soul with her eyes.

Without saying a word, she put the glass down and held up her purse. She looked at herself in the reflection provided by the highly polished leather and made sure her hair was in place.

"Grandma gave me this shiny purse because she said I could see how beautiful I was."

I wanted to laugh at the preciousness of her statement but managed to squelch it to a broad smile and respond, "The purse is Grandma's way of helping you see your own beauty."

Elinda smiled and nodded.

"It must really be precious to you."

She nodded again.

"What's in your purse?"

"Oh, just some Kleenex that Mom said I might need and some barrettes and some pennies and some crayons and a picture."

It was the picture that I intuitively felt was important to see but I asked about the crayons first in order to make looking at the picture a more casual event. "What colors of crayons do you have in there?"

One by one she took them out. "I've got red—cause that was Grandma's favorite color—and blue, for the sky—and yellow, for the suns around angels' heads—and green for the pretty grass."

"Wow, you have your own little color supply store in there, don't you?" She nodded soaking up being the center of attention of an adult who wanted to fully see her and was intent on being completely present with her.

"Whose picture do you have?"

She took the picture out of her purse. "It's a picture of me and Grandma at my last birthday party. Grandma's the one in the red dress with the <u>black</u> belt." Her clarification was precious because, while she and Grandma were both wearing red dresses, no explanation of the other figure was really needed.

"I wonder if it would be helpful for you to draw a picture of Grandma in her new home. I have some blank pieces of drawing paper here and you can explain what you are coloring as you go along."

It was amazing to me how readily Elinda took to this task and the mixture of profundity and childish understandings that she brought to it.

The first thing she drew was a great big wonderful sun right in the middle of the top edge of the paper with rays emanating from it. At the bottom of the paper, she used kelly green to draw a grassy pasture. The main figure, Grandma, was, of course, dressed in red. She was, according to little Elinda, standing at a table making homemade pasta for the big supper she was having with the "polar bear angels."

That puzzled me but I figured I would wait for her to begin to draw the "polar bear angels" to see if that would help me better understand what she meant. As it turned out, the "polar bear angels" did look like polar bears except that they had yellow wings and little yellow circles above their heads. All of the ursine angels were depicted, in childlike fashion, as sitting around the table at which Grandma was making the pasta.

"Can you tell me more about the "polar bear angels?"

"You know, <u>the</u> polar bear angels—the ones that carry Grandma to God."

Now it was clear to me! There was confusion between the pallbearers and the angels she must have been told accompanied Grandma to her new place. To a small child, who has never heard the term "pallbearer" before, it could, if said quickly, sound like something exotic with which she was more familiar: "polar bears."

"Oh, yes the ones that make sure she is safe in her new home." I decided not to try and explain since that was not the primary issue. "Grandma looks very happy in her new home but I don't see you in the picture?"

A dark shadow fell across her face. "That's because I wasn't invited 'cause I was too little." She began to cry silently and big tears welled up in her eyes and fell in her lap. I felt like hugging her and rocking her to give her reassurance as I would my own daughter. But I resisted that intervention and gave her a Kleenex as I said, "Oh, Elinda, I feel so sad with you. It must really hurt to feel you couldn't be part of Grandma Elinda's good-bye."

She nodded and began to sob audibly. At that point I reached out to her and touched her upper arm and rubbed it gently and slowly. I had a daughter about her age—transference anyone?—and it was very painful for me to see someone my daughter's age, like Elinda, cry so hard.

Following my own intuition, I waited a little while before softly saying, "Would it help if we had another good-bye celebration for Grandma just for you?"

Elinda looked up at me and again searched my eyes to see if I really meant it. Then she nodded.

"Well then, that's what we'll do. We'll gather all of your family and Grandma's friends and we will go out to where Grandma's buried. I will wear my robe—because I am the priest—and we will have another good-bye service for Grandma. Afterwards, we can sit around the table just like the "polar bear angels" and remember Grandma while we eat. Do you feel that would help you feel better and sleep better and be able to grow to be the same beautiful person Grandma loves so much?"

Elinda nodded, wiped her eyes, dabbed at her nose and then asked for more Hi-C. As she drank her Hi-C I asked her what her favorite things were about Grandma Elinda. All of the memories she then shared with me would be helpful in making a rite of passage ceremony specifically for Elinda at the gravesite.

When Elinda's mother came to pick her up, I invited her to sit down with us so we could share together what we had planned. I told Paula, while Elinda agreed, what we felt would be helpful and mentioned many of the things that were significant memories of Grandma. I asked Paula if she could call around among her family and friends and gather as many as she could at an agreeable time at the gravesite for another short funeral service. Afterwards, I continued, it would be helpful to Elinda if there was another funeral dinner complete with the kind of pasta that Grandma used to make.

"Maybe Elinda could even help make the pasta," I suggested. Elinda's face lit up with that idea. Paula agreed to call me as soon as she could poll the family members.

I shut the door behind them as they left saying to myself that I didn't have a clue if this idea would work. This was twenty years before I came across Murray-Bowen's family systems theory and its concept of the almost unique ability of clergy to intervene in helpful ways in such important moments as marriages and births and funerals. I do not recall being aware, at that time, of the notion that a family is a living, organic "being" which is as profoundly affected by the addition or loss of a member as one would be if he or she were to lose an arm or grow another ear.

The concept that all of life is connected and that the famous statement, "A sparrow does not fall to the earth without your Father in heaven knowing" might be more of an indication of our organic social wholeness rather than a protection from suffering, was not even a glimmer to me at that point in my life.

At any rate, it felt like the helpful thing to do. Yet it was so outlandish I was afraid to ask the psychiatrist who taught the pastoral counseling class about it or even mention it to any of my fellow students. Going to a graveyard to have another funeral service in order to rid a suffering family member of the feeling of being disconnected from the living as well as the dead, seemed less than respectable in a rational world.

When I told my wife, in vague terms to protect privacy, with her usual forbearance of my crazy ideas, she listened carefully and said, "That's nice dear." Her response reminded me of what she said the day we went fishing for bluefish our in Long Island Sound. She had shown me up by catching the largest blue that day and winning the joint pool of funds collected from each passenger to go to the one who caught the biggest blue of the day. I expounded, in great detail, upon the bigger blue fish I had hooked but was unable to land. She had said then, too, "That's nice dear."

The day of the second funeral service at Grandma Elinda's gravesite was sunny and just a little brisk. Five year old Elinda and her siblings had helped her mother make the pasta for the dinner following the service. They used the same kitchen tools that Grandma had used and followed her recipe. Paula and Elinda both shared with me how proud Grandma would have been to see the results and how close they felt to Grandma when they were making the pasta.

I wore a black robe to the graveside service because it was the only robe I had. The service was a shortened combination of a regular funeral service and committal service. Paula had managed to gather about 40 relatives at the gravesite for this re-creation. It must have taken some powerful persuasion on her part to convince the people of the efficacy of what they were going to take part in. Then, again, it might just have been the promise of Grandma Elinda's pasta that was the draw. Whatever it was, I was grateful so many came.

In the short homily, I touched upon all the things that Elinda had mentioned to me as being special about her relationship with Grandma. Grandma loved to read stories to Elinda and hold her on her lap as she did so. Grandma loved to have Elinda help her in the kitchen and always asked Elinda's opinion about how things tasted when they came out of the oven.

Grandma would let her dust the expensive crystal and polish the silver candleholders. Grandma would have Elinda spend the night; they would watch old movies together and eat popcorn until little Elinda fell asleep. Grandma would brush Elinda's hair and tell her how pretty she looked especially after Elinda had discovered how to dress up with Grandma's old dresses, shoes and hats from the 1920's in the attic.

I closed the homily with this prayer:

Dear God

We thank you for Grandma Elinda Montario;

We know she is as special to you as she was to us;

Our faith is that she is now enjoying herself in her forever home with you;

We are going to miss her terribly—the hugs and
secrets and cooking and laughs.

Remind us that Grandma is not completely gone
from us
But is present when we make her food recipes,
When we treasure the gifts she gave us,
When we share her laughter,
When we recall her wonderful smell as we crawled
up in her lap
And she read to us.

Thanks for connecting her to us with our memories
and our family
Who helps us keep the memories alive as valuable
gifts.

Thanks for the tears we shed for Grandma
And for the smiles we share about her.

Remind us, now and always, of the wonderful
things that come from
Beginnings as small as a seed or a memory
As tiny as a smile

And as warm as the food we share as a family.

This we ask in the name of Jesus
Who lives to keep us connected with Grandma
And each other,
By the power of Spirit,
Through the will of You who made us. Amen

The meal we had afterwards was wonderful. There were Grandma's stuffed shells and homemade spinach bread. There was Italian wedding soup and a bounty of goods I cannot now fully recall. They are, however, probably still part of me.

Little Elinda was in her element with her patent leather purse and red dress serving up stuffed shells as the guests filed down the buffet table. Grandma Elinda may not have been there in body but she was surely there in spirit, thanks to those polar bear angels.

Elinda stopped wetting the bed. Her temper tantrums subsided. Her moodiness dissipated. The last time I contacted Paula, three years afterwards, Elinda was doing fine. It's less of a mystery now than it was then in as much as I at least have a theory about why it worked. Still, there is mystery in it. Maybe that's the point.

Chapter Two

Right Field Ronny

Ronny was on the verge of being a lost boy. His mother had died two years before I met him. Her absence, in small town, traditional gender role America could be seen in his wrinkled clothes and often dirty face. The degradation of want had not pierced his soul for his angelic expression and quiet forbearance drew me to him.

His father, in a battered old pick-up truck, would come to his son's little league games and watch while sitting in the truck in the nearby parking lot. After awhile, I figured that Ronny's Dad never came to sit in the bleachers with the other parents because it restricted his choice of beverages. Having a brew while watching a ball game is a time honored, American tradition: "apple pie, hot dogs, cracker jacks, never get back." Ronny's Dad took it to the point where he could benefit from a stay in an institution for "drying out." That did not prevent him from loving his son the best he knew how.

Because Ronny was a big kid, he wasn't quite as coordinated as some of the other players. Nor was he blessed with the gifts of a natural athlete. His attention span was short. His nerves hadn't grown quite yet to reach and communicate with his muscles. Picking flowers and chasing butterflies while playing right field came as naturally to Ronny as the blessing of the sun to the verdant fields on a spring day.

Yes, I was ashamed of myself for putting Ronny in right field. Every little league baseball fan knows right field is a kind of "institution" in its own right. Right field is where you put the players who haven't quite got the hang of it, who aren't ready, developmentally, to focus, whose skills are behind those of the other players. Right field is for those players who require all of the attention of a coach if they are going to contribute to the team and get any better. Right field is for those who need remedial help.

Right field was where Ronny was positioned the day we played the best team in the league. The previous season they hadn't lost a game and were the champions. Their coach had been managing for twenty years and, because of the relationships he had built up over his tenure,, had the leverage to pick the best athletes among those who came to the elementary school gym for the annual "draft' of talent. He often knew the older brothers and sisters of the new players and had scouted those who were the best "prospects" in the "developmental" league, T-ball. George Steinbrenner would have been proud of the man for making a kids' game into a cutthroat business.

As the newest coach in the league—and definitely a wayfarer as I was serving two small, marginal country churches—I did attend the annual talent selection. No attempt at assessing a player's abilities was made the day of the draft in the school gym. I was simply handed a list of fifteen boys and girls, eight and nine years of age. One name looking as good as any other to me, I thankfully received the list of names and phone numbers, eager to share the feel of a well-hit ball, the smell of a new glove, the delight of racing around the bases.

These were the experiences that the players of the league's best team were raised with. In contrast, when I tried to expound upon the excitement of the bat, the ball, the bases, my players looked at me as if I were another one of those adults trying to convince them they would understand someday. Yet, somehow on that day we faced the best team, we played as if we were personally illustrating the hackneyed idea "that on any particular day….."

The score was very close; we were ahead by two runs in the bottom of the sixth in a six inning game! They had a girl at second base and one of their better hitters was up to bat. Ronny was in his own little world out in right field, picking the clover flowers and throwing them up into the spring winds to see if he could catch them before they were carried away. This was his usual game day behavior.

But he seemed to have a personal itch problem that day that added a new wrinkle to his fielding regimen. In fact, the amount of time he spent scratching himself was making serious inroads into his enjoyment of the carefully mowed monoculture of the outfield. Being distracted from his usual distractions made Ronny, in my mind, an even more likely candidate for a fielding disaster.

With a loud, metallic clang the ball flew off the bat high into the air toward right field. Poor Ronny had his hand down his pants trying to attend to his personal itch. The opposing side's fans erupted into loud hosannas. Our bleachers were silent, the sound of the parents' sucked in breath swallowed up by the anticipatory tumult of the other side.

Simultaneously, we all shouted, "Ronny, look up, look up!!" His father was in his truck, parked right along the fence on the sideline of the right field. No more than fifty feet from his son, it was probably the sound of the truck horn and his dad's voice that got Ronny's attention. He took his left hand out of his pants and raised his gloved hand to shield his eyes from the sun. From the way he scanned the sky, it was obvious he had no clue where the ball was. All he knew was that it was coming his way.

Ronny was getting exasperated. He took his glove away from his eyes, turned his head toward his dad's pick up and spread both of his arms out toward his father as if begging him for more clear direction. At that precise moment, the ball plopped into his glove. It had to be the most providential act ever witnessed in a little league right field. But this was just the opening scene.

The runner for the other team, undoubtedly convinced that Ronny would never catch the ball, was around third on her way home. Ronny's father was honking his horn and yelling at the top of his lungs, "That's my boy! That's my boy!" My frantic gesticulations must have finally moved him to realize the drama was not over. He joined us in loudly directing his son to throw the ball to second base in order to get the runner out, end the inning and win the game.

The throw that Ronny made was not pretty. In an older, less genteel time, one might say he threw like a girl. But the throw did reach second base, our second base player was on the bag expecting it and corralled it into her mitt. I did not notice if our second base player took her foot off the bag before the umpire signaled the out. Our whole team was swallowed up in the giddiness of victory. We had not tasted it that year and were glad to be drinking that nectar so addictively sweet it is blinding.

I did notice the coach of the other team conferring with the umpire after the game but thought nothing of it; I was not invited in on it nor told of the subject. I was wrapped up in the congratulations of Ronny and building him up. And we were all in a hurry to get to the local ice cream outlet and get that free cone provided by the owner.

As the season wrapped up, that game was the only one that we won and the only game the other team had lost. Their coach protested the outcome saying that our team had broken the rules by prematurely leaving the field before the umpire had called the runner out at second. I never knew of the protest or of the meeting where it was considered until it had all been decided. All I received was phone call informing me that the game had been rescheduled to be played again from the first inning.

I dreaded the day of the game. It was hard to convince our team that the rules hadn't been stacked against us. But I kept up a brave front, exhorting my team that we had beaten them once, we could beat them again. Inside, I psyched myself up to be on high alert to pay excruciatingly close attention to every aspect of every play so that those with inside connections couldn't snatch victory from us again.

I need not have worried. There was no doubt about the outcome of this replayed game. They led by five at the end of the first inning and the game was called in the third inning because they were more than ten runs ahead. I did shake hands with the opposing coach only as an attempt to promote sportsmanship among all concerned. To this day, I think what was done was outrageously unconscionable.

This is the first time I have every told this story. I have always been concerned that if I were to try and tell the story publicly I would become sputteringly angry. It still rankles and reiterates, in a small way, the nature of community power structures in small town America. Those with inside connections too often make the rules, interpret the rules to their advantage and decide, behind closed doors, upon any questions about the rules before those who are just passing through ever know what has happened.

The team picnic we had after the game was a leaden affair. The players would ask why we weren't allowed to replay the game just from the second out in the sixth inning. Why did we have to replay the whole game over? I could only reply that I didn't know why. The parents of the players asked the same question. I tried to explain about the nature of community power relations. Their glazed over eyes indicated that a more immediate, visceral kind of answer was expected.

Ronny's father got so drunk at the team picnic that I had to drive him and Ronny home. I helped the poor man into his house and made sure he was in bed with a bucket available. Ronny said he had food and would be okay just watching baseball on television. I gave him my business card and said that maybe we could play catch sometime. Ronny smiled and nodded in a way that indicated it would mean a lot to him.

Forgive me, Ronny, for never making it back to play catch. Forgive me for not being able to mobilize children's' services and other community resources to help you more. Forgive me, for not calling out the other coach on his deceitful power play. Forgive us, for placing you in right field.

Chapter Three

"SANTAFYING" CAPITALISM

Ministry in rural churches has its joys. There is the fresh produce in season and the fresh meat after helping load hay. The people are often straightforward, hard-working and unhomogenized in the sense of being unique characters. Social pressures to conform don't take the same shape as in more populated subcultures, so all kinds of unique individuals happily abide in rural America and its small towns.

I may have belonged to that group the year I decided that, to raise money to provide my family with Christmas gifts, I would reprise the historical character, Saint Nicholas. To recount the story of the original Saint Nicholas: he was the Bishop of Myra, in Turkey, in the fourth century of the Common Era.

Bishop Nicolas was very well off and generous. When the news reached him of three girls who would not be suitable marriage material for they were too poor for a dowry, he threw bags of gold through their window at night saving them from not only a penurious life, but, perhaps, a demeaning one as well—or so the story goes.

The primary difficulties were two: I was hoping to convert the legend into bags of lucre for my family and, second, venues to perform the *shtick* were few and far between. I could not imagine a way of recruiting an audience to watch a recreation of the role of Saint Nick without portraying the three girls saved from a life of debauchery in the costumes of such a lifestyle. Why pay to see Saint Nick when you can see him for free at a mall?

There it was—at a mall. The nearest mall was 25 miles away but gold fever beckoned me as strongly as it motivated the '49ers. I hopped in my 15 year old car and drove "more rapid than eagles" to the management office of said mall.

They seemed quite impressed that I was willing to surrender my ministerial dignity to a red velvet suit with glued on eyebrows. I was impressed with the fact that they were willing to pay me $10 an hour—over twenty years ago that was equivalent to $20 an hour today. Not making enough money to safely avoid food stamp eligibility, this seemed like an especially good deal.

I had a blast trying to reincarnate the spirit of joyful giving of Saint Nicholas. It was especially fun to ride up and down the escalators, with my elf holding the basket full of candy canes, at the department stores bellowing, "Ho, ho, ho, Merry Christmas!" My voice was well developed from preaching and leading congregational singing over the years so everyone—from the managers to the workers to the shoppers and their children—could hear good old Saint Nick no matter where they were in the stores.

Those children who were not terrified—and I cannot remember many who were—stood in awe as I passed out the cellophane covered red and white swirled candy canes and invited them to come and see me and my helper so we could visit about what they wanted for Christmas.

Just for fun, I made sure to give each store mannequin we passed its own candy cane. One of the managers asked me what I was doing so, staying in character as Saint Nick, I laughed my "Ho, ho, ho" and responded that the figures, so stiff during store hours, come alive after everyone is gone. I pointed at the floor and continued that she could see evidence of this in all the empty cellophane wrappers on the floor every day. She smiled and walked away shaking her head and chuckling to herself.

My *shtick* was working! I was actually spreading joy by personifying Saint Nick in the local temple of materialism. This made me feel a little better about using my interpersonal and dramatic skills to help mere merchants capitalize on the story of a saint. My mind rationalized that this was just another kind of ministry especially if I worked with the right spirit and a convincing portrayal of joyous wonder and imaginative generosity.

The children were wonderful! I had gone to special pains to be sure I looked the part of Saint Nicholas. I used my own latex glue to attach my white eyebrows. Even though my uncorrected vision is 20/440, I did not wear my glasses. Children responded to me with wide-eyed innocence and awe as if I were the man himself rather than just a poor country preacher who was trying to help myself out by giving Saint Nick a hand. They didn't seem to mind that, with fifty pounds of padding, a red velvet suit and smelling slightly off due to the sour smell of the latex stage glue, Saint Nick's odor was not always holy.

Most of the children had at least one gift on their minds when they sat on my lap to talk with me. The gifts ran the usual gamut of dolls and action figures and trucks and tricycles. Some had made good old Saint Nick cookies which I gladly accepted—but never ate—and crayoned pictures of Rudolf, their dogs, their families, their houses, a layout of their house pointing out where the fireplace and the tree were located, etc.

One 7 year old child, from a more formal setting, even had a calling card with her printed name and address and her list handwritten on the back. She was leaving nothing to chance and left my lap saying, "If you have a hard time finding my house, just call and my parents will give you directions." The best response I could make in that age before cell phones and GPS was that I remembered her house from the previous years I had dropped in and would be sure that Rudolf had her address.

There were, of course, always sad things that children shared in their innocence with Saint Nicholas. The adorable, blue eyed brother and sister who sat together on my lap asked me to make their parents stop fighting and yelling. Choking up, I could only stammer that I was watching their parents and would remind them to be nice rather than naughty when I dropped in Christmas Eve. That seemed to give the two little ones some comfort and hope and they left as satisfied as I could make them in that setting with that proscribed role.

Not one child left a wet spot on my lap. Only a few were so terrified that it was all their parents could do to coax them to stand beside my "throne" long enough to have a picture taken by the elf. I did my best to tone down my voice for the frightened little ones and make myself as small as I could with my body posture to be less threatening. The elf usually managed to get one picture in which the poor little scared child was not actively crying although a few were caught still sniffling.

When word got out—probably through those elves who should have been back at the North Pole workshop rather than gossiping about Saint Nick—that I was divorced, it became *de rigueur* for the available female mall workers to come by and visit with Saint Nick. One middle-aged worker even asked the elf to take a picture of her on Saint Nick's lap. What she wanted for Christmas is best left between her and the Saint. Fortunately, she did not draw any pictures.

One beautiful young woman—and I could squint well enough to see that she was comely even in my blinded, glassless state—seemed particularly attracted to the personality of Saint Nicholas. The second to last day I was scheduled to be Saint Nicholas, she boldly approached and plopped herself on my lap. There was only one thing about her presence that I couldn't figure out: something white that I couldn't make out at twenty feet was trailing behind the heel of her right shoe. I did surmise that my elf had gone to the bathroom and this young woman had deliberately waited until she would be the only one in line and no one else was present—except a multitude of passing shoppers.

I was nonplused by the directness of her approach. With my glasses on and in my street clothes I was the guy who one night asked 13 women to dance and got turned down 12 times. The only female who would condescend to be seen dancing with me that storied night was 35 years older and took pity upon my ineptness. I had never experienced myself as a hot item and did not know what to do as myself let alone as Saint Nicholas.

What would Saint Nicholas do, I kept asking myself nervously, as she wrapped her arms around my neck.

"I want a date for Christmas," she purred.

"Uh-h-h dates are kind of difficult in this part of the world. How about some fig newtons?"

She pressed a piece of paper in my hand, kissed me on the cheek and said, "Give me a call, Santa."

I looked down at my hand and finally noticed what was trailing behind her right shoe heel: it was a piece of toilet paper! As discretely as I could, I tried to reach down with a free hand and grab it without her noticing reasoning that only the one who loves you would risk telling you there was mustard on your face; everyone else would pretend it wasn't there. I did successfully manage to snag the toilet paper but not to avert her gaze. Her cheeks turned crimson red and without a word she flew, "as dry leaves before the wild hurricane fly" off my lap and walked away without looking back. I disposed of both the toilet paper and the paper with her phone number on it. Not even a saint could resurrect this situation.

I was sorry to see the last day I was to work as Saint Nicholas come to a close. I had to leave promptly at 4 p.m. as the parish I was serving had a tradition of having a Christmas Eve communion service and I still had some preparations to complete before the service.

A knock came at the door of the storage room I used to change from my street clothes into my Saint Nicholas costume. Without waiting for me to answer the knock or calling to see if I was dressed, in came my favorite elf, April, a young nursing student. I had already taken off my beard, ripped off my fake eyebrows—taking some of the real ones with them--but still had on my red velour pants with the suspenders that held them up.

April pressed herself up against me, put her arms around my neck and kissed me on the mouth.

"You are a rebel and I like that."

"I enjoyed working with you, too," I stammered.

"I want to give you your Christmas gift tonight—and tonight only."

"Tonight only?"

"Yes, this offer," she continued as she ground her pelvis against mine, "is good only for tonight."

This was really tempting. April was a very gorgeous blond with great posture and a beautiful smile. I was no longer Saint Nicholas but just Keith Rasey sorely tempted to blow off my responsibilities to my congregation and go to the nearest hotel for a Christmas tryst. My mind was racing. If I went to the hotel with her, I would be dishonoring the spirit of the ministry I intended to embody as Saint Nicholas and be in danger of letting my congregation down. On the other hand…it had been a long time since I had been with a woman.

Awkwardly, I took April by her upper arms with my hands and gently pushed her away. Where the strength came from to turn down such a delicious offer, I do not know. At the moment part of me thought I was doing the wrong thing and part of me felt I was doing the right thing.

"I can't tonight, April. I have responsibilities in my job that I dare not ignore."

"I understand," she responded.

I gave her one more hug while kissing her on the forehead and wishing her Merry Christmas.

That night, as I served communion, I thought of what God had given up at Christmas and wept.

Chapter Four

SINGING UPSIDE DOWN

Some ministerial wag once said to me that he learned to develop great compassion for the wealthy because it paid better than empathy with the poor. I have never been able to get past my own version of Maslow's famous "hierarchy of need" scale. The neuroses of the well off do not seem as urgent as the basic needs of the truly poor for food, clothing and shelter.

My heart is always open much wider for a poor person just trying to survive that day than to a member of the upper middle class struggling to pay their child's tuition at an exclusive private school. This has been a mixed blessing in my work with parishioners and community members.

David Clinton, for example. He was one of the most bedraggled, beaten down human beings I had ever met. His right arm was withered and I would later learn it had been that way since birth. Misaligned teeth filled his mouth and his one eye was on a focusing track far afield. It says a great deal about how my children were accustomed to all kinds of people showing up at the front door of the parsonage that my oldest son, Joshua, even opened the door.

"Uye wud sijk ysemding du aet, please," is what he said to Joshua.

I know that's what it sounded like because he repeated the same thing to me when I arrived at the door. It took all of the empathetic resources I could draw upon—reading his facial gestures, his body language, his hand movements, the pacing of his words in a southern drawl—before understanding began to dawn upon me. The translation was, "I would like something to eat, please."

This was a common request from strangers at the door of the manse. And I had created an on-going arrangement with an avuncular member of a local Greek Orthodox Church who ran a nice family restaurant, The Prince's Tavern, near the church I served. The going rate was up to $10 for supper and $5 for either breakfast or lunch for anyone who presented my business card with my handwritten request on the back. Of course, I would not pay for cigarettes or beer or liquor.

Once or twice a week I would stop by to eat and pay the tab for the indigent wayfarers who had stopped in.

Sometimes, if there was any money available, I would use the pastor's discretionary funds that were collected in a specific offering plate when people came forward, during worship, for monthly communion. But usually I paid for it out of my own pocket.

The idea was to give people what they wanted when they showed up on the front porch of the manse. I had learned a long time ago in seminary, when working with those who were not in any way part of my parish, to just give what was asked for. To try to do more was to over function in a way that the person being helped might find humorous as they did when, early in my ministry, I tried to help a family with more than they asked for.

The mother had called me on the phone and asked for food assistance. She shared it was just her and her fifteen year old daughter in the household which was only 3 blocks from the parsonage. I asked her if she needed any toiletry or sanitary products and, when she responded they were okay with what they had, I wrote down her address and phone number and said I would be by later in the day.

When I knocked on their apartment door my arms laden with a week's worth of groceries, the woman greeted me at the door with a "Hello, Father" and smiled (this was a heavily Roman Catholic neighborhood and not many made a distinction between a priest and a Protestant minister; it didn't bother me and actually saved me from getting mugged a couple of times). She had one very lonely tooth suspended from her upper jaw. But what really took me aback—it was all I could do to not stare—was the severe crocodilian overbite of the fifteen year old daughter. She would have been a perfectly acceptable looking teenager except for that more than toothsome display.

I kept my composure and said the obligatory, "You're welcome" and noted I would stop by the next week to make sure they were doing okay.

My heart went out to the daughter. The furniture in their apartment was late Salvation Army with a dollop of Goodwill. There were no lampshades on the floor lamps. Their television was a small black and white with wadded up foil on the coat hanger that served as an antennae. It was clear they could not afford dental care, I reflected to myself.

So, later that week, I called around to find out what kind of free orthodontic services were available to the indigent. The mother and daughter hadn't asked me to do this but it just seemed only right that they would want the girl to have that overbite ameliorated especially as her poverty included so many other deficits she had to overcome.

I finally found out that the Dental School at the University of Connecticut in Storrs offered low price, based on income, orthodontic services. I asked a wealthier member of the church if she would pay for the services needed--$800 at that time—and she agreed. That settled it then. I was willing to drive them up to Storrs, I had secured the funding and now I only needed to announce the triumphant news to the family.

It was a great feeling as I bounded up the stairs of their apartment that day and tapped melodically on their door. I could only imagine how grateful they would be to me for removing this hindrance to the girl's successful social adjustment and achievement.

After asking how the food was holding out, I got to the point: "I couldn't help but notice your daughter could benefit from braces."

There was an uncomfortable silence in return. The woman just kept smoking her cigarette and looking at me with a steely glare.

"The University of Connecticut at Storrs, " I plowed ahead, "has a dental clinic just for situations like this."

More silence and smoke.

"We would be happy to drive you up there and pay for anything needed." I was deeply puzzled by the woman's lack of responsiveness and by how still the daughter had become. I kept quiet and let the silence build its own pressure for her to make some kind of response.

"That's kind of you, Father," she finally said. "Leave us your phone number and we'll talk it over and get back with you."

I did give her my business card and reiterated the offer and suggested, most earnestly I am sure, that this would be really helpful to her daughter's health and well-being. She nodded as she ushered me out the door.

I had taken no more than two steps out of their front door when I heard them erupt in laughter, the kind of laughter that is best described as hooting and hollering with knee slapping thrown in to relieve pressure. They never did call.

Giving David Clinton, therefore, what he asked for was what I was going to do. It was not only easier, it was also probably the right thing to do for it did not arrogantly assume I knew better what he needed than he did. Nor did it make me responsible for fixing his life. I am not God. To give someone a stone when they ask you for bread is not a very loving—or helpful—thing to do.

Mr. Clinton was just another in a long line of people that I had fed or clothed or transported or helped with utility bills or aided with medicine or drove to hospitals to see sick relatives. I learned to never expect them in worship or to become a part of the churches I served. I grew over time to realize the goal was not about changing them, but an opportunity for me to demonstrate, in concrete actions, the love of God. With precious few exceptions, the folks who the churches I served assisted through my ministry didn't bother to disabuse me of the notion I would never see them again.

David Clinton was to be different. He actually showed up for worship the next Sunday morning! He had even combed his hair and taken a shower. His presence was a real gift to the congregation because when he was there at least the place was integrated—a little—by race.

The oddest thing was not the fact he was black and the rest of the congregation white. The strangest thing was that David could not read! As he sang along with the opening hymn, he held the hymnal upside down the whole time just to make it look like he knew what he was doing! The poor guy had to be in his thirties and he was illiterate.

Showing up for worship gave me a greater responsibility to develop a relationship with David than if he had just been one of the multitudes who had shown up to be fed. I became an expert at his language and soon he did not have to repeat himself for me to understand him.

As I learned his story I felt deeper and deeper empathy for him. David was from the Deep South. He had been born with a withered arm. He had no formal schooling for he was told he was not capable of learning to read. When the institution he was living at shut down, a large metropolis in the South had put him on a bus promising to buy him a bus ticket to anywhere he wanted to go. He chose Manchester as his designation because he had a vague memory that was where his grandmother was from. The local YMCA had let him have a room in exchange for his help with janitorial work.

An entire legion of angels could have been kept busy helping David with his multitudinous troubles. I honed in on the most basic ones such as income and a job. He should have been eligible for Social Security disability but he did not have a Social Security card. I called the county seat where he said he was born and managed to obtain a copy of his birth certificate.

We marched down to the Social Security Office and picked up a Social Security card. The case worker there signed him up for disability income. When that arrived, the church helped him rent a small, inexpensive two room apartment. I managed to find him a job working as a laborer—of sorts-- at a trucking company. A couple of times I even took him to work and picked him up when he called saying he needed a ride home.

If felt wonderful to be able to help someone such as David. It is said that some fortunate people are born on third base and think they hit a home run when they become a success. David was born with two outs, two strikes and a broken bat in his hand. Just being able to stand in the batter's box is a remarkable achievement for him. He was grateful.

If only the story would have ended there. Flannery O'Connor wrote that the moment of grace incites the devil to a frenzy. While I do not believe there is such a supernatural being as the "devil," I do believe the moment of hope is also the greatest time of temptation. David's case bears this out.

Coming home from a hospital call, I drove up the alley behind the church as I always did to travel to the nearby parsonage. Strange lights were flickering on the tall stained glass windows of the church. I pulled into the parking lot and saw two police cars parked there. When I opened my car door, I heard the burglar alarm wailing. Hurriedly, I used my key to enter the back door of the church near the kitchen.

"Don't move," a voice commanded as a flashlight was shone on my face from across the room.

As my eyes acclimated to the darkness, I could see the blue steeled glint of a gun barrel and a badge. I heard the low growl of a big, big dog. Instinctively, I put my hands up in the air. Life really does imitate art, at least the "low" art of television crime shows.

'I'm Rev.Rasey," I said authoritatively. I was determined not to get shot by mistake.

The policeman asked me for identification. Using my church keys, they then began a systematic search of the entire building. This was not an easy task for it was a huge, neo-Gothic facility with all kind of nooks and crannies in which to hide. After a few moments, they found the entry point at which the intruder had broken in and gave the firemen access just in time to prevent the place from burning down. Whoever had helped themselves to access had also helped themselves to some lawnmower gasoline and was trying to create his own personal Pentecost with fire for everyone.

The firemen put the fire out quickly. It didn't take the dogs long to track down the intruder, either. He was cowering in the Youth Room in the basement, next to a large television he was trying to pilfer with just one good arm. It was David Clinton!

Twenty years of surprising disappointments in ministry had not prepared me for this! At least the fire was small and contained. The television was not damaged. David, however, was in the city jail.

That night he called me on the phone from the jail. He was crying and blabbering and going on in such a way that, deprived of the clues given by facial gestures and body language, I couldn't make out what he was saying. So, at one o'clock in the morning I got out of bed and went down to the jail.

The guards, who knew me from my regular trips to visit in the jail, let me meet with David even at that early hour. He cried and cried and apologized and apologized. Having lived in an institution most of his life, David did not have a whole lot of experience with street drugs. He said he had been given some PCP and he just went crazy for more and more. I promised to show up at his arraignment and do what I could for him. I held his hands in mine and prayed for peace and insight, courage and hope, for both of us.

The next morning, I called the church attorney and prevailed upon him to do what he could to have the criminal justice system treat David with as much kindness as possible. David did not have a criminal record. Since he didn't drive, he had fewer encounters than I did with the police.

Plea bargaining was a wonderful thing for David. The church attorney was able to plea down the sentence. David got thirty days and court costs, which I made him pay out of his last paycheck.

The last I saw of David was at the Greyhound Station. He wanted to go to a small town in Georgia where there was a group home for people from his former institution. I had called to check the place out and it seemed to be on the up and up. I agreed, then, to pay the bus fare and give him money for some meals on the way.

I hugged him tightly before he left. He cried; I cried. Were the tears more for me or for him? I am ashamed to admit some of the regrets were personal. Why was I so privileged and poor David so needy? I may not have been born on third base, and I may not have two strikes on me with two out in the bottom of the ninth. But at least I can read the trademark on the bat.

Chapter Five

THE IMAM AND WINE PONG

"God is one." I just nodded my head in agreement to show that I was listening as I sat on a chair to his side.

"God cannot be three for how can the infinite be divided without losing its unity?" he continued as his fierce eyes challenged mine. The linen turban on his head was immaculately wrapped and his robes were a combination of grays. I refused to rise to the bait.

"Therefore, any Trinitarian formulation for the being of God is not only wrongheaded, it is also apostasy."

"Apostasy?" I thought to myself. Did he really know who these kids were? They were from my confirmation class at a church in a rural farming community. They may have had some knowledge of epoxy but that was about as close to apostasy as they ever got.

This whole hypnagogic scene was my responsibility. I had always made it part of the educational experience for members of the confirmation classes I taught to visit a synagogue, a Roman Catholic Church and/or monastery, if possible, and an Eastern Orthodox Church of some kind. Over the years, it became possible to add a visit to a Hindu temple, as more were being organized, but this was 1981, the year of the very first visit to a mosque by a confirmation class that I taught.

This mosque was the largest one in the United States and, reportedly, outside of the Moslem world. It was in Dearborn, Michigan, also, supposedly, the largest concentration of Islamic adherents outside of the Moslem world. It was a broadening experience for the members of the class to just travel to such a metropolitan area since the town which was the seat of their county only had ten thousand residents. It is quite possible there were more farm animals in their county than people. The census takers only counted the two-legged residents so no one really knew.

The structure of the mosque was very impressive although we were not given a tour of the sanctuary. In recent years, when mosques have deliberately became more receptive to non-Moslems in order to promote tolerance and establish some understanding of the commonality of belief among the three major monotheistic religions, Judaism, Christianity and Islam, a tour of the sanctuary was always included as long as we took off our shoes.

"So, you understand," the Imam continued in slightly accented English in 1981, "since God is one, we can recognize Jesus as a prophet, but we cannot worship him. Are there any questions?"

The youth who were witnessing this supposedly erudite instruction of their ignorant pastor were between twelve and fourteen years of age. Their questions would be existential: when was lunch? I know they had barely heard of the Trinity. They were not prepared to debate the finer points of the Trinity any more than I was going to be inhospitable when raked over the coals for the philosophical errors of Christian doctrine.

We all breathed a sigh of relief when the Imam rose, said his good-byes and we left for lunch.

Subsequently, I have had some wonderfully hospitable-- no debates--visits with confirmation classes to mosques. For example, there is a mosque in Perrysburg, Ohio, whose minarets erupt like volunteer sunflowers in a field of wheat, which has a magnificent sanctuary with the ninety-nine names of Allah inscribed on stained glass windows around the top of the worship area. After the tour and a short explication of the major tenets of Islam, they serve a magnificent Lebanese meal. The tour became, for me, such a routine part of my year that the highlight of each visit was the baklava. Salivation replaced any and all concerns about salvation.

Gustatory concerns were always as the heart of my ecumenical experiences. Food is such an intimate part of the spiritual experiences of the *hoi polloi* that sharing the repasts of the Hindus, various Eastern Orthodox denominations, the Jews, etc. became as much a part of the instruction of members of the confirmation classes as learning the books of the Bible. Baklava may have done more for interreligious understanding than any synod or conference.

But food can also be divisive as far as what it symbolizes in ritual. It was my privilege to participate with a Roman Catholic priest, in Bridgeport, Connecticut, in a joint Roman Catholic/Protestant wedding at the Roman Catholic sanctuary. Of course, there are some substantive differences relating to the serving of communion. Roman Catholicism's official doctrine is that the communion elements are the very body and blood of Jesus the Christ while Protestants typically adhere to the belief that Jesus the Christ is spiritually or symbolically present in the wine and the bread.

What made it more difficult in this particular situation is that the church I was working with did not use wine, as the Roman Catholics did, in communion, but grape juice. It is the Roman Catholic practice to be sure that none of the wine is wasted so, after sharing communion by intinction i.e. the dipping of the bread in the wine, the priest would usually drink the remaining wine. This presented quite a problem to me as I wasn't much of a drinker.

It wasn't so much that I was morally against wine and spirits as that I had no experience with them. I had once been invited to a party at the house of a prominent physician in New Haven in which strolling musicians—several groups of them—journeyed throughout his mansion playing for the guests. There was an open bar so, having a Scottish last name and wanting to be hospitable, I ordered a Scotch and water. I am sure it was a high quality Scotch, but to me, with an undeveloped palate and a tongue not used to such high octane titillation, it might as well have been gasoline.

The first sip I took set my throat ablaze and singed my vocal cords on the way down. I quickly made my way to the nearest bathroom and dumped most of this expensive tongue anesthesia down the drain. I left just enough in the glass to color the large amount of water I substituted for the Scotch a caramel hue so it looked like I was joining in the festivities. The Scotch was much more bitter than the hectoring lecture of the Imam in front of the confirmation class.

I always went to great lengths to fit in the best I could in order to practice the grace of hospitality, which is one of my spiritual gifts.

So, acutely aware of the necessity of practicing hospitality as a sign of the presence of God in any relationship, I was keen to do the kind and right thing at the joint marriage ceremony with the Roman Catholic priest. He was going to serve communion to the Roman Catholics present at the marriage ceremony and I was going to serve communion to the Protestants. I had brought my own brass chalice and the priest used his parish's chalice.

I thought nothing of the fact that the priest filled the chalices to the top with communion wine. It was his place and whatever he did I had committed myself to not only approve but imitate as a sign of our unity. The bread was dipped in the wine for each person who came forward for communion. One hundred and fifty pieces of bread can soak up a lot of wine compared to the less than fifty pieces I served to the Protestants present. I had a lot more left in my chalice than the priest did.

When all had been served, as was his tradition's custom and belief, the priest drained what was left of the communion wine in his chalice and placed it on the altar with a flourish. To be straightforward, I cannot recall, beforehand, thinking much of what he would do with the left over and what I would do with the left over wine. This was my first joint Roman Catholic/Protestant wedding and I had given far more thought to the more ethereal aspects of ecumenical hospitality than to the practical aspects of cleaning up.

I tried to imitate the priest and drain the large amount of wine left in my chalice. He didn't seem to have any trouble gulping it down so I took a big swig and immediately gagged and coughed. My face turned red and I cleared my throat several times. I recovered my composure and took another huge gulp which resulted in more sputtering and gagging and consternation.

With a look of utter theological disdain, the priest authoritatively grabbed the chalice out of my hand, quaffed the remaining fluid down with one smooth swallow and resolutely placed the chalice, with the resounding ringing resonance that only solid brass can make, upon the altar. Snickers tittered throughout the congregation.

I had never felt more like a theological wimp in my entire life! It seemed as if my spiritual mettle had been tested and found wanting. I wanted to pull my robe over my head and slink off to the sacristy like the poseur I was. An ancient and theologically sophisticated version of the game of wine pong had broken out and I had lost.

Years have passed, since then. I still do not have a taste—or even a tolerance—for Scotch, no matter how refined and expensive. But I have learned how to drink wine without gagging and continue to hope for another opportunity to imbibe the spirit of religious cooperation and tolerance. It may even be true that wine pong proficiency may be a necessary theological condition for ecumenical cooperation.

Chapter Six

MEPHISTOPHELE'S FIRECRACKER

"Husky" was the word that could be used to describe Daniel. He wasn't fat. He was just big all over. At the time I was working with Daniel and his family, the boy was twelve years old. He had a close haircut that was called a "butch" when I was his age.

Like Daniel, I wore a butch and was "husky" when I was twelve; I even wore clothes that carried that size designation from a local department store. I wasn't quite sure, at a tender age, how that word related to sled dogs but did know it was somehow kin to "lard ass" which was what my Dad called me.

Dad was emotionally distant. He was working hard to climb the ladder of corporate success. My mother provided most of the "hands on" parenting—including both the discipline and the tenderness. In my gut, I knew there was more than a little similarity between the emotional atmosphere of Daniel's household and my own family of origin.

Daniel's dad struggled with alcoholism. He worked as a welder at a local ship manufacturing business. I had read that the fumes given off by the lead used in some types of welding could cause serious physiological consequences.

Historically, welders have used alcohol to handle the lead fumes that accumulate in their bodies. I am not sure about the biology of it all for lead is not miscible in grain alcohol. But like the "mad hatters" who suffered from mercury poisoning in Lewis Carroll's day, drinking was a stratagem that kept these men alive in a less-than-ideal working environment.

Daniel's mom worked as a teller at a savings and loan in the community. She was a very positive person—the type of woman that I would encounter again and again in my work in parishes. Her corporeal heaviness seemed to be a means of compensation for a life without much gratification or pleasure. The public breeziness that she presented as an inherent part of her character was, in itself, a means of handling the tremendous underlying pain of her life. Another way of saying this is that her public persona was more of a role than an authentic part of herself.

Her mother, Daniel's grandmother, lived with her daughter and son-in-law. Daniel's live in grandmother was also quite pleasant although, in her case, this pleasantness was a means of handling a slowly growing sense of befuddlement as the cataracts of aging sagged upon her faculties and character.

Having grandmother in the same household was a means for the family to save money, provide for all concerned and have a reliable, at home childcare provider when needed for Daniel and his younger brother. The emotional price for all this, however, was more than the prevailing rate for babysitters because Daniel's mother was parenting her own mom, Daniel, his brother, Brent as well as her husband.

When Daniel's mother would unburden herself to me, her public persona would rapidly deconstruct. She would begin to tremble as if she were losing her ability to maintain her own emotional equilibrium. Her visage would change and settle into something like the tragic mask that, in the theater, personifies tragedy. Carole's physiognomy plummeted into a chiseled expression of grim, frozen realities.

The struggle to maintain a more composed and pleasant countenance, alone, would drain the emotional energy reservoir of anyone who had to engage in relationships with her inner world and the world at large in order to make a living. With all the responsibilities that rested upon her broad shoulders—and they needed to be wide to carry her burdens without physically collapsing-- the psychological energy to hold her life together and face the portents that even a small change in her family might cause, had to be exhausting.

I empathized with her innate understanding of what she must do and who she must be to emotionally balance the relationships in her family. Her husband spent too much of his considerable wages on alcohol. He had alcohol "investments" all over his home and work. Bottles of hard liquor were purchased and ensconced in safe places. The emotional energies that might have more helpfully been invested in parenting his children, caring for his wife and providing for his household were drowned by the dark compulsions of his disease.

Complicating the situation, at least for twelve year old Daniel, was that he was named after his father. Not that Daniel Senior was an evil person in any outward sense. He was in regular attendance during Sunday morning worship. He was always nicely dressed in a dark suit and tie. Senior didn't snore loudly during the service. He didn't reek of alcohol. When he greeted me in the morning service and at church potlucks, he was always cordial and socially acceptable. What it cost Senior to present himself as perfectly in charge of his own life in terms of emotional resources, I could only wonder.

The sadder issue was that Daniel Junior was being taught similar kinds of "coping strategies" by his parents. The entire affective ocean in which the boy "lived, moved and had his being" was poisonous. He imbibed unhealthy adaptive behaviors with his first taste of mother's milk. I wonder how many generations of his ancestors had also been taught to engage in such similar behaviors. Therapeutic interventions with Daniel Junior and his family would have likely had to move against the staunch flow of a "cloud of witnesses" whose behaviors had become somaticized even in their descendants.

All of this was forgotten for the Fourth of July. In New Haven, the Fourth of July is a major percussive event. The entire street from curb to curb of the block on the street of the church was covered with "silver salutes." At midnight on the third of July, to explosively open the festivities of the Fourth, the complete sequence of intertwined fireworks was set off, saluting the dawning of the Fourth with a fiery hello.

My family was invited over to the house of the Lay Leader, Hal Balogh, for a picnic the evening of the Fourth. Hal lived in a neighborhood that prided itself on its blue collar, ethnic origins and pretensions even though most of the residents had long since either moved into management or were comfortably retired.

To say that Hal was in management was a kind of double entendre for he also had to manage his poor wife, Elaine. Elaine had once experienced a complete mental breakdown and was just a shell of the person she had been beforehand. She was as close to being in a state of suspension as I ever seen someone who was not institutionalized. Elaine moved slowly and deliberately. She never looked anyone in the eye and seemed to have her eyes perpetually fixed on a spot on the ground about ten feet in front of wherever she was at that moment.

After a pause, when spoken to, she would reply with a flat voice. Her words were always a relevant response to what the conversation was about but her affect was as inappropriate as a corpse at a circus. Hal made all the decisions for her. He was in charge of her life completely. A cross between a parent, a nurse, a companion and a "minder," Hal enjoyed the freedom to do as he pleased. His girlfriend was more convenient that way.

It was difficult for me to ascertain if Elaine's behavior was because of her medication or because she had been completely depersonalized by her husband or some combination of the two. One of the unfortunate side effects of her drugs was that she had lost her femininity. She didn't care what she wore and her clothes, although clean, were often twenty years out of date. Hair grew profusely but at widely separated places on her face. The wispy hairs were very white against her ruddy complexion and so quite noticeable. No effort was made to remove or control them.

The surrender of her freedom had terrible consequences for Elaine and, although he couldn't acknowledge them without the dawning of a devastatingly critical self-awareness, for Hal as well. His house was immaculately in order but his home was a shambles. There was all the furniture one could find in any home; there were pictures on the wall, a television in the living room. But the atmosphere was somehow as sterile as that of an outdated theme park in which things were too perfect to be real and too off the mark to be productive fantasy.

Hal was quite a kingpin in the local church that was part of the two-point charge I served. Puffing on his Chesterfield cigarettes, Hal would preside at church meetings like a mob boss. His mien was frozen in a forever frown. Nicotine smoke clung to him like sulfurous fumes from Mephistopheles. His was the kingdom and the power and the glory forever.

Hal's pogroms ranged from the mundane, like who scribbled in crayon on the church woodwork in the chapel, to the serious, such as what to do about the bullet holes newly created in the church kitchen cupboards. When he adjudicated his decision, any discussion was considered over and in poor taste.

As my wife and daughter got ready to leave the manse and go over to Hal's for his annual Fourth of July party, I wondered what kind of machinations would be required as payment for my presence. Was Hal going to conduct a campaign to get rid of the bilingual daycare? Was Hal going to announce a new effort to work more closely with neighborhood leaders aka minor organized crime participants? Was he going to loudly proclaim his alliance with those who wanted to sell the parsonage and use the monies for sanctuary remodeling? Was he going to trash other church members in my presence trying to draw me into some kind of public confrontation? Who knew what danger awaited me there? I did not realize that it was dangerous for others as well.

Hal had provided ladyfingers and sparklers for the children. There were also more dangerous fireworks for the bigger "kids."

One of the bigger "kids," Daniel Senior, lit an M-80, equivalent to a quarter stick of dynamite, and threw it away from a group of people who had congregated on Hal's lawn. There was, of course, a window shaking boom and then a world shattering scream of pain from the knot of people.

In the dark it was difficult to see who had been struck and who it was that was bent over at the waist clutching their hands to their face. As I drew closer, it became clearer: Daniel Junior was bent over in terrible pain, moaning. Something had entered his left eye.

We laid him on the grass and someone ran to call 911. His mother, Carole, comforted the boy as best she could and asked for a flashlight so she could look in his injured eye. Those who had been in the house came out to the front lawn and stood as far away as they could in such a small city lot, talking quietly, and cringing a little more self-consciously now at the continuing sounds of revelry around them.

The local fire station, only a block away, had an ambulance on the scene in less than two minutes. Paramedics quickly sized up the situation and loaded Daniel Junior into the ambulance for the trip to Yale New Haven Hospital. I volunteered to drive the rest of the family to the hospital but Daniel Senior, seemingly composed, wanted to drive the family himself. I still wonder to this day what he and his wife talked about on the way to the hospital.

I took my own family back to the manse and drove myself over to the hospital. Finding Daniel's family, at night, in such a big city hospital was not easy. I finally found them, not in pediatrics, but in the general surgery section. The ophthalmologist had been called, Daniel was sedated and the family had been told to wait in an isolated corridor.

I really didn't know what to say or do. The previous week, an elderly receptionist at the hospital had told me, when I came to visit a parishioner, that I looked like a teenager. I felt like one then. The obvious thing was to ask if they had seen Daniel, what he had said and what the medical personnel had said and done. In other words, just to let them tell me their stories.

I did know enough to ask open-ended questions such as, "Where were you when you found out Daniel had been hurt?" The question of what had caused this to happen to his eye was too awful for me, a mere twenty-five years of age myself, to ask.

What I did know to do was listen carefully. This I did as well as I could with good eye contact and attending behaviors such as nods of the head and guttural sounds of having heard and understood, "uh-huh, um-muh, hm," etc what was being said. I focused on the feelings behind the words being conveyed.

Those feelings were hard to identify. Years of hiding genuine feelings in an ingenuously contrived persona geared toward day to day survival and the utter awfulness of what the alcoholic father had done, accidently, to his namesake, increased the forces that buried emotions. After all had been said that was going to be said, I suggested we pray together. We held hands in a circle and closed our eyes to focus on that which wasn't readily apprehendable in that institutionally blue hallway:

"Creator God,
Who watches over the littlest and least of all creatures,
Watch over us and your beloved son, Daniel.
It is so hard for us to know what to say
For we are numb.
We thought we were going out for just a holiday
And this has fallen upon us so
Quickly

We have been stunned.

We do know, and have faith, Lord

That you are working in our lives

And in the skills of doctors and nurses

In this place of healing

To restore Daniel to wholeness.

Let him know we are here with him and

That you and we will never abandon him."

There was a short pause as I waited with my mind
centered in my heart for what was to be said next. As
always, the words were given to me:

"The waiting eats at us.

We wish we could do more.

We wish we knew what needed to be done

To make this situation all right.

While we wait,

Hang in there with us, Jesus,

As you choose to hang with all humanity on a cross.

Share our burden,

O, Crucified God,

Grant us, and Daniel

Comfort.

Console

Us with the hope that just as surely as you were

Crucified,

Were you also

Resurrected.

Walk along with us

As we travel this great darkness

Until we can see the

Hope

Of how you yourself, personally,

Will help us handle this.

This we ask,

Beseeching

You

Pleading

As your own children who place our trust in you as

the Great Physician,

the Good Shepherd,

and the God of never ending goodness.

Amen.

The prayer was cathartic. Daniel's mother and grandmother were crying. Daniel Senior just looked at the floor and swallowed hard. Little Brent, only eight, didn't quite know what to say or to do or where to look. I was emotionally wrung out from the ordeal of having to wrestle with the angels mediating healing words, phrases and images.

Another, more important caregiver, the eye surgeon, came around the corner. What he shared with us was not what we had hoped to hear. Daniel Junior's eye had a foreign object of some kind in it. The object, according to the surgeon, seemed to be on its edge so he wasn't able to determine how deep it had penetrated into the eye socket. He assured us that Daniel was sedated and comfortable and in no pain. But the doctor was going to have to operate to determine what the object was and if vision in that eye could be saved.

When I looked the eye surgeon straight in the eye and wished him, "Godspeed," he seemed to recognize what that meant and accept me as a fellow healer for he thanked me and turned and left. This was the very first time I can remember being accepted by a physician as a fellow member of the care team. It validated my services and helped me feel that I was providing something not only wanted, but medically needed.

There was a short silence. It was determined that grandmother and little brother would go home to go to bed. It was, by now, two o'clock in the morning and the operation was estimated to take at least two hours. I volunteered to drive the two home and the offer was accepted.

On the way home, I made small talk with little Brent about his little league baseball team in order to give him some time to relax and rebound. The intensity of such an experience for a person with the emotional equipment of an eight-year-old had to be overwhelmingly tiring.

Grandma seemed even more removed to the past than usual. She talked about what Yale New Haven Hospital was like when she went there to have her daughter, Carole. She reminisced about how much smaller it was then. She mentioned that then the neighborhood around it was better. She didn't touch on her hospitalized grandson. It seemed that grandmother needed a breather, too.

I made sure they were safely at home and went to the manse for a minute myself. I relayed to my wife, Marilyn, what had happened so far. It was going to be one of those all night vigils and I wanted her to know where I was so she could be reassured. Michelle, our daughter, was fast asleep in her own idyllic world of Winnie the Pooh and ballet costumes.

I arrived back at the hospital around 2:45 a.m. The lady at the night desk gave me the usual hard time about looking like a member of the clergy. She said I looked like a teenager with my blue jeans and casual shirt and shoes. I showed her my clergy identification badge half feeling she was right. I did not look a day over 17 and wondered, myself, what I was doing there. I had that common, awful feeling that I was an imposter and was soon to be found out. But I kept going to the corridor where I had last seen Daniel's family. Not a soul was in sight.

So, in those days before cell phones, began the oft played game in a large metropolitan hospital called, "find the family." I had long since learned to use the pay phone to save steps. I called the hospital, told the operator who I was and who I was trying to locate. She rang the surgical waiting room. There were no members of the family there. She rang the regular waiting room. No family members there, either.

I suggested she call pediatrics and that did it. The ward clerk said the family was in Daniel's room resting as best they could and waiting for him to come back from surgery.

I stopped in the chapel on my way to the elevator. The large Bible on the altar had been opened to Isaiah's words:

Those who wait upon the Lord

Shall renew their strength;

They shall mount up with wings

 Like eagles.

They shall run and not be weary;

They shall walk and not faint.

The scholar's debate about whether the messianic Servant Songs in Isaiah are to refer to an individual or a community or a group of individuals within the community came back to me. What a struggle it was to be true to what the best scholars had discovered about the Bible and the needs of persons straining for some kind of hope to hang onto throughout a personal crisis.

Lost in such thoughts, the ride in the elevator to the tenth floor went quickly. I walked into Daniel's room. There was Carole but no Daniel Senior. He had gone to the cafeteria for some coffee. After a half hour watching the only channel still broadcasting at that hour—this was before cable—Daniel Junior was wheeled into the room.

There was, as expected, a large patch over his left eye. He had an intravenous bag on his IV pole. He was groggy but glad to see his mom. I said I was glad he was back in his room and the surgery was a success. I was careful not to say too much.

Carole quickly broke into tears and said how sorry she and his Dad were that this had happened. She reminded him that it was an accident and that his Dad had taken the precaution of throwing the thing in the opposite direction. I contributed that I had seen his Dad light and throw the firecracker and he had, indeed, thrown it away from everyone.

Daniel himself asked the obvious question about where his Dad was. Carole replied he had gone some time ago to get coffee from the cafeteria and should be back by now. I volunteered to go on down to the cafeteria and take a look around. Carole caught me halfway down the hallway and asked me to check and see if their family car was still in the same lot where they had parked when they arrived. I knew what she feared and said that I would do as she asked.

I couldn't find Daniel Senior anywhere around the cafeteria. The few people there said they hadn't seen anyone who matched his description. I went out into the darkness and the uncertainties of the neighborhood at three o'clock in the morning to check the parking lot. Their car was gone. The father had taken off. Carole and I were both concerned that he would do something to hurt himself.

The first thing I did was to find a pay phone and call a person who I knew was very actively involved in the local Alcoholic Anonymous circles. The poor guy answered the phone with a mouth full of cotton and words slurred with sleep. I relayed that I needed to get in contact with Daniel's AA partner so I could find Daniel. This was urgent in order to be sure he was all right as there had been a terrible family accident and the family was afraid Daniel would hurt himself.

My friend understood and knew exactly what to do. He told me to wait by the payphone and he would contact Daniel's AA partner and have him call me. The hope was that the AA partner could tell me some places David might go when he went on a drinking binge. Fifteen minutes passed and then twenty. Thirty minutes later the pay phone did ring. A deep voice identified himself as Ralph, Daniel's AA buddy. He asked me if I was Rev. Rasey. I answered affirmatively and said I needed to find Daniel because I was concerned he might harm himself in his guilt about an accident that happened to his son.

Ralph was a helpful as he could be. He said there weren't any legitimate bars open at that time of day. There were no twenty-four hour liquor establishments open, either. The best thing to do was to check out the donut shops and the brothels. Ralph also knew that Daniel stashed away liquor for just such occasions and that the mother lode was his own property. He volunteered to go with me. We arranged to meet in the waiting area of the emergency room.

At that time of day, the nighttime rush of a big city hospital emergency room was over. The persons who sought treatment for shootings and stabbings and heart palpitations and car accidents and spousal abuse were now gone. The interns were grabbing some sleep. Nurses were catching up on their paper work. A single custodian mopped up a stubborn, congealed bloodstain.

It wasn't hard, then, for Ralph to find me. We used my car to drive to the donut shops that were still open. Mostly they were populated with policemen trying to stay awake and alcoholics trying to sober up enough to wander home.

Ralph suggested one more place—an afterhours "nightclub" he called it. It was a nondescript looking central city house except for the red light on the outside of the door. He knocked twice. There were two knocks that came from within and Ralph knocked three more times. The door was opened. There was a breathtakingly beautiful redhead with a see through peignoir.

"Welcome to Madam's," she said.

Ralph replied, "Thank-you."

I concentrated on keeping my eyes focused on the eyes of the women who were making themselves available in their various stages of undress. There were many beautiful moving objects and I was using all of my willpower to keep focused on eyeballs. The red velvet flocked wallpaper and the lamps with strings of oil descending around the dim light bulbs made it easy to characterize the décor as urban brothel.

"Have you seen Daniel, tonight?" Ralph asked the woman who had answered his knock.

"No," the beautiful creature replied. "He hasn't been here for a long time. Would you like a drink and a date?"

Ralph easily replied no. I just blushed. That was like waving a red flag at a bull.

"I bet your friend would like to have some fun!" she purred.

I stuttered that I was a minister.

"Sure, you are honey. And I am a mother superior. Whatever floats your boat we can provide."

"No, really, I-I…" Ralph put his hand up to shut me up. "We'll just be moving along then."

"Okay," she responded. "See you in church."

Ralph decided it was so late that even a man on a bender would seek the safety of home so he drove to Daniel's home. Sure enough, Daniel's car was in the driveway. Ralph pounded on the door until grandma came and let us in. There was Daniel, on the couch, with two empty bottles of cheap liquor on the floor.

"I guess he's safe for tonight, " I remarked to Ralph.

"Yes. for tonight," he responded.

Carole called work for Daniel Senior the next day to say he was sick. His work had already paid for Daniel to be dried out once and they would fire him if he went off the wagon again.

The next Sunday, Daniel Senior was in church as usual and acted as if nothing was wrong. I told him, in the receiving line after the service, that I was praying for him and his family and said I would do anything to help them. He mumbled his thanks and kept going.

Daniel Junior did recover from losing his eye. He was proud of his black velvet eye patch and excited when his new prosthetic eye came in. He graduated from high school and took up computer programming at a local community college. His Dad kept his welding job but as far as I know, they never attended another Fourth of July celebration.

As for why all this happened at Hal's, an evil spirit did seem to surround him. What about my misgivings about the possible machinations Hal could subject me to? Perhaps Hal had been practicing genuine hospitality. Even the worst person has some good in them and the best, some evil. Or perhaps Hal didn't have enough time that evening, with all that transpired, to carry out his latest attempt at spiritual terrorism on me. Keeping others up in the air as they dealt with the concussions of the booby-traps he set up was Hal's principle means of entertainment.

It is exceedingly odd, though, that such an explosive event with so many emotional ramifications occurred at Hal's place. There is a folk belief that the emotional realities one carries inside—and the consequences they produce—follow one around. Hal was not so evil as to wish what happened to Daniel Junior and his family upon them. But he did cast an almost sulfurous pall on the people around him and the circumstances they shared with him. Perhaps, in this respect, the fact that Daniel's family experienced all this at Hal's house was no accident after all.

Chapter Seven

FUNERAL DATING

"Cow number 109 is looking better and better, "I said to the head of the personnel committee of the church I was serving as pastor.

"I would have to say," I continued while he smiled, "that she is utterly beautiful."

He laughed easily and nodded as if he, a long married man, understood.

It was bad enough that an inquisition was launched by the church hierarchy when the mother of my sons decided to divorce me. She averred that I was a good minister but a terrible husband. It was miracle that she was willing to say anything nice about me but hoping for another miracle—someone my age to date—seemed to be too much.

I had a meadow behind the parsonage that was filled with cows who had numbered ear tags. They were the only available females my age in the entire town.

"Why would I want to pick up another man's socks for the rest of my life?' an eighty year old widow noted when I asked her about her dating life as a single person in this small town. "I did have a man who came over to ask me out but he pressed down on the wrong pedal in his car and ruined my garage door."

There was no internet dating then. I couldn't very well hang out at bars without word getting around to the parish. Where would I find someone both available and near my age? At a funeral, of course.

The deceased wasn't even a member of my parish but a relative of a prominent member. There was nothing extraordinary about the calling hours except for one striking, fairly young female who was a niece of the deceased.

A raven haired beauty whose décolletage was prominently displayed, her outlined lips and shadowed eyes looked better than cow #109. She had great posture and knew how to carry herself with the skill of someone who was familiar with being on display. This did not occur to me, at the moment. I was overtaken by the presence of someone who noticed me while I was noticing them.

The funeral service and committal at the graveside were not anything really different than the hundreds I had conducted before. Except for this bereaved morsel who wore a black hat, with a brown feather, and a slinky black dress that made her the best turned out mourner I had ever seen.

"I am sorry for your loss," I said to her as I left the graveside. She pressed her hand in mine, hugged me and pressed into my palm a piece of paper. People in the past had given me checks this way but this was, in my desperate state, an even more munificent communication: her phone number.

"Is this Chastity?"

"Yes, of course," she answered. "Who do I have the pleasure of speaking with?"

"This is Rev. Rasey. How are you doing?"

"Oh, I am getting by. I am glad you called."

"Really?" I said incredulously and innocently.

"Yes, I was hoping to hear from you."

There was an inept silence as I thought about how to proceed. Chastity seemed to be leading and I was just following along.

"What are you doing Saturday nite?"

"Nothing I can't get out of."

"Great. Let's get together to eat. I'll buy."

"Okay," she responded. "Where are we going?"

I hadn't thought about that. This seemed to be moving faster than my own, too long pent up imagination.

"How does George Palmer's House, sound?" This was the nicest, and most expensive place I could not afford, I could think of.

"I haven't been there for awhile so that is wonderful."

"I'll pick you up at 7:00." I said my good-bye and hung up.

The only problem was I neglected to ask where she lived.

"Chastity," I began on the call back, "where do you live?"

She laughed and gave me her address. Then we were all set.

Wow, I thought I actually had a date for the first time in three years. I was a little uneasy about how this all seemed to be more in her control than mine but I eased my anxieties with the old saw that beggars can't be choosers.

What was I going to wear? I had funeral suits, go to meeting suits and not much else. I figured this was neither a funeral nor a worship service so I didn't know what to wear. I opted for my most casual go to meeting suit with no tie. As I apprised my appearance in the mirror before leaving to pick Chastity up for the evening, I looked neither funereal nor too holy.

Chastity was dressed as a knock out. Her blue dress was cut six inches above her knees and about two inches too short to adequately cover her chest. She may not have been able to raise the dead but she certainly sparked my interest.

"Is that your Harley in the garage?" I asked as I tried to make small talk on the way to the restaurant.

"That belongs to the father of my son." At least it wasn't hers.

"Is it fun to ride?"

"It used to be."

I got the feeling we were talking about riding something other than the Harley.

"Is it comfortable for long trips?"

"As long as it doesn't rain, snow, the bugs don't get in your teeth and the guy you are riding with doesn't strand you at a gas station."

I did not want to go there. "I have only ridden a motorcycle once in my entire life. And it did not stop at any gas stations so I will take your word for it. "

We spent the rest of the way to the restaurant talking about her son and my sons and sharing notes about being parents.

"Smoking or no smoking?" the maitre d' asked.

"Smoking," she said before I could reply. This was a woman who was used to speaking for herself. It was news to me that she smoked but I was willing to overlook any vices if she was willing to overlook the fact that I picked her up in a ten year old station wagon.

She sashayed behind the maitre d' and, I am not ashamed to say, I watched and followed along. We arrived at our table too soon.

With a flourish, the maitre d' placed our napkins in our laps, opened the menus and handed them to each of us.

"Please order whatever you would like," I said, trying to sound hospitable and magnanimous. Secretly, I hoped she didn't order the lobster.

"I don't care for lobster so I think I will order the Alaskan crab legs with asparagus béarnaise and red skin potatoes." She then pulled out a carton of Marlboro cigarettes, tapped one out and looked at me as if it were my obligation to light her fire.

Fumbling with the matches provided, I managed to strike one up and hold it in front of her as she leaned forward toward the flame. I had seen Humphrey Bogart do this in the cinema but had no personal experience.

"So, you know what I do for a living, how about you?" I ventured.

There was a short hesitation. She took a long draught on her Marlboro, blew the smoke out to her right side, evenly met my eyes with hers and responded, "I am a party girl."

What did that mean, I asked myself. Was that the same thing as what Steve Martin, then au currant, said when he described himself as a "wild and crazy guy?"

The blank look on my face gave her an invitation to continue.

"I work on Park Avenue in Brooklyn."

It took time for that to register for me. I knew Park Avenue was full of strip parlors—and I am not talking about furniture refinishing here—but didn't immediately know how this related to Chastity.

"Chastity is my stage name," she added.

I didn't know what to say, so I said nothing.

"Monique is filling in for me tonight so I am free."

I hope she didn't mean free as in no charge for it was becoming increasingly obvious to me that this was not going to work out despite the expensive meal and my interest in her.

"So your real name is....?"

"Evelyn."

"I could see that Evelyn would not be as fetching a name, nor as helpful as Chastity, in your line of work."

"Yea, most men are pigs and do not want reality to intrude too much into their romantic life."

I didn't know if I was supposed to oink or squeal. I changed the subject.

"What made you decide to smoke Marlboros?"

"I like cowboys."

The salad came to rescue me from having to immediately respond.

"I remember when I was a kid," I said when the conversation seemed to have come to a dead end, "really getting into Roy Rogers and Hop Along Cassidy."

"Who?"

I might as well have mentioned the names of their horses. She was talking about hard living, hard riding and hard drinking men who fancied themselves as modern cowboys: wham bam, thank you ma'am types. Remembering my youth with my double six gun holster and cowboy boots was not relevant.

"Never mind, "I replied. "What is it about cowboys that attracts you to them?"

"They seem to be real men in an age of so many girly men." Her eyes were sizing me up. Good thing my suit coat covered my flabby abs and untoned biceps.

"Not too much call for vocations for cowboys in Cleveland. I haven't seen a herd of cattle in these parts, ma'am, for at least 150 years." I smiled to let her know I was trying to make light of this.

"It's not what they do for a living. It's the way they treat a woman and live their own way."

"Sort of like the image of Harley riders."

"Yea," she responded not getting the connection I was making to her history with her son's father and her misbegotten image of real men. It was obvious that this delectable creature wore all of her virtues on the outside and was more artificial sweetener than substance.

Once again, the arrival of food broke up the mood. Crab is a great meal to have when you want to have something to do when the conversation is leading to a parting of ways. Cracking crab legs and digging out the meat provided a neutral subject to talk about and concentrate on.

I prayed that she did not want desert and my prayers were answered. At least some of my prayers came true that night, I wryly noted to myself.

"Well, I guess I'll take you home," I said after we had decimated the crab.

She excused herself to use the restroom and I had a chance to look around. A cursory glance of the room indicated there was no one there I knew. I only hoped there was no one there who knew Chastity/Evelyn and could place me in her presence. I could hear the gossip in my mind, "Preacher takes stripper to dinner." I wondered if I could get away with saying it was a modern avatar of Mary Magdalene although I am pretty sure that no one would ever confuse me with Jesus.

The question, "What would Jesus do?" had not dawned on popular consciousness. I was stuck with thinking about what I should do. It was obvious I was not her type—thank you Lord—and the best thing to do was pay the bill and depart as quickly and as graciously as possible.

The ride home was uneventful. I resisted asking her about her work and she resisted lighting up another Marlboro in my car.

I never picked up another woman at a funeral parlor or, more accurately, allowed a woman to pick me up. Of course, another beautiful woman has never pressed a paper with her phone number into my palm at a funeral, since.

But now I have learned how to deal with it. Cow #109 is a great listener.

Chapter Eight

FREQUENT FLYER

There are events that happen in life that are just too astounding to fully understand. A parishioner stops you in the grocery store on the spur of the moment and gives you $500 cash to help with the expenses of your newborn baby in the hospital. An older member of the church, in front of her boyfriend at her house, takes off her bulging blouse to proudly show you her heart surgery scars. Your dog sneaks into the church you serve, nearby the parsonage, and leaves a theological statement in a scatological form on the carpet in the third grade Sunday School room.

An ordinary phone call from a community member sobbing as she asked me to visit her four year old son who was in pediatric intensive care in Yale New Haven Hospital was not, in the overall structure of my work, so odd.

"He's so innocent and undeserving of this," she sobbed.

"You feel this is not fair," I replied softly.

"No, it is-s-s-sn't. What did he ever do to anyone?"

"What is your boy's name?"

"Stephen, like the first martyr."

"I'll stop by to see him this afternoon."

"Please hurry, Father. He is on a ventilator and might not last long." I could hear her continuing to sob as I hung up.

How sad, I thought to myself: a child the age of my daughter on a ventilator, hanging between this life and whatever life there is to come. I rearranged my afternoon schedule in order to see Stephen first.

When I checked in at the nurse's station on pediatric intensive care to find out what bay he was in, the nurse at the desk gave me an odd look as if she was wondering how I got swept up in all this. I felt as if I were auditioning for a role in a drama she knew all too well but worried about my ability to inhabit. I wrote this off as another example of people put off by my looking too young to be a minister.

Stephen was indeed on a ventilator. He was very light skinned boy whose veins were easily seen through his skin. When I looked closer, I discovered he was developmentally disabled with distinctively oval eyes. I prayed silently for him, pleading that he not be in pain or suffering, hoping for the very best outcome for him and those who love him, praying that God would find a way to make this turn out to everyone's benefit, when I heard a soft clearing of a throat behind me.

I turned around to find a comely young black haired woman behind me. Her hospital name tag said she was Rachel and was a Psychiatric Social Worker. She introduced herself and I replied that I was Rev. Rasey.

"How did you get entangled in this?"

"His mother called and asked me to visit."

"Is she a member of your church?"

"No."

"She never is," she responded softly.

"What do you mean by never is?"

"You don't know much about Stephen's mother, Gloria, do you?"

"I've never even met her."

"She probably likes it that way. We see her here every two or three years with another disabled child she has adopted who is dying. She's one of our frequent flyers."

Those words stunned me.

"Yes," she continued, "she is reprising the same role she has played no one knows how many times."

"It's the same ending every time?"

"Yes. She is unable to have any children of her own so she adopts terminal disabled children no one else wants, mothers them for a few years until they become too sick and the drama closes here."

"Why does the state keep allowing her to adopt them?"

"She passes the background check and home study. She and her husband are very well off and she doesn't work outside of the home so she has her whole life to devote to carrying for the terminal children she finds."

"So, she does something to kill them and they still give her others?"

"No, no, no. This has been thoroughly investigated by the state and there is no abuse going on. In fact, she does an exemplary job juggling their medicines and doctor appointments. The children are always fashionably dressed and well taken care of. "

"Why would anyone subject themselves to this, again and again?"

"Some would call it a variant of Munchhausen by proxy, although in all of her cases she doesn't do anything to cause harm to the child. The harm is inherent in each child's disease process."

"But in Munchhausen by proxy the caregiver seems to be relatively unshaken by the hospitalization and Gloria was quite broken up by Stephen's being in pediatric intensive care."

"Yea, that's probably how she keeps getting away with adopting terminally ill children. It's not that they don't suffer as the illness develops its normal disease process, but she doesn't cause it and is always emotionally torn up by it, as well."

"So she is hurting herself over and over again by reliving the dramas of the children she adopts dying?"

She nodded.

"I don't think that all that grief is healthy. There is something not right about choosing to pick at the same emotional wound again and again."

"We agree and I have tried to raise it with her but she just gets mad and walks away muttering that we don't understand."

"From a Karma perspective, I wonder what she did in past lives that she is atoning for now."

"That would be fascinating to know and might even help stop this merry go round upon which we are role players. Every time she brings us another child I hear the calliope music playing and wonder when this circular, pointless—and emotionally painful—journey ends for all of us."

I thought about what the Social Worker had said as I drove home. This was a weird case. How do you help someone whose whole life work seems saintly? Not only that, she didn't want any help and saw what she was doing as living selflessly for others. She was Mother Theresa without the convent.

Is causing emotional harm to one 's self necessary in order to serve others in the name of God? Vincent Van Gogh had been kicked out of missionary work in the Borinage region of Belgium, working with coal miners, because he gave up his comfortable bed for a miner suffering from black lung disease. Van Gogh slept in a doorway. The missionary association did not consider Van Gogh emotionally balanced enough to continue in ministry. He was causing pain—and perhaps disease—to himself in order to help his sickly neighbor.

The difference is that Mother Theresa saw her work as bringing glory to God by serving God in the very form of the poorest of the poor. This service brought life and meaning to Mother Theresa because she saw herself as sharing the sufferings of Jesus when she shared the sufferings of this world's "nobodies." Who did Gloria see herself serving? What did these children represent to her? Why did she not adopt children who could have the possibility of having a more normal lifespan?

The commandment says to love your neighbor as yourself. How is it loving to love a child, again and again, who you know for certain will die? That seems more like subjecting yourself to continual heartache and emotional suffering. It is one thing to accept the possibility that your child will die. It is quite another to choose children who you know will die without a doubt.

I called Gloria that night.

"I would like to visit with you to offer you emotional support and get to know you better," I said into the phone.

"That would be lovely, Father, but we are so busy what with my husband's business and my Stephen being in the hospital. How about if you meet me at 1 p.m. at Stephen's bedside tomorrow? We can talk some, then."

I agreed.

Gloria turned out to be a slightly plump woman in her late forties. Her round face was dominated by a pair of protruding eyeballs. Her motions were quick and her hands were always in motion.

I hugged her as I would have anyone who was losing a child.

"Any change in his condition?" I asked her.

She shook her head no and began to sob softly.

"This really hurts."

She nodded again.

"Would you like to pray?" I asked as the attending nurse came into the room.

"Would you like to join us in prayer, nurse?" I asked. She demurred with a smile but as she left the room she caught my eyes and rolled her own in their sockets.

I asked Gloria to hold one of Stephen's hands while I held another. Gloria and I joined hands to complete the circle. This prayer was going to be edgy because I wanted to address the continual recurring scene in this room with Gloria and a succession of children.

"God of many names

We are not wise enough to understand why this

continues to happen to Gloria.

Her love for her many children is

Strong

Gentle

Complete

Boundless.

Thank you for the grace you have given her.

Release her from this round of suffering

Comfort her

With the whisper

"Well done my good and faithful servant,
Now enter into the reward of your master."
May your approval finally save her from suffering
without end.
As for your son, Stephen,
Grant him ease of breath
Peace of heart
The physical embrace of your presence
In our touch, our kisses our hugs.
Remind us, he is just a temporary gift from you to
us
So Stephen might know we release him
From his sufferings
And commend him to you
Who has made him and awaits
To reclaim him
As your own.
Heal our memories of so many times we have stood
here
Waiting
For the final healing to come.
Grant us the grace to lay aside our
Guilt,
Our incompleteness,

Our emptiness,

To make room for you to create new life without

end

In and through us now

And forever.

In the name of the One who once shared our mortal

coil

And sanctified it with goodness and joy and

lightness of being

In this life and in all the life that is to come. Amen."

When I opened my eyes, I found Gloria's staring into the face of Stephen. The hand she had used to hold Stephen's was caressing it. She kept saying, "my baby, my baby" over and over. My prayer was as therapeutic as mere aspirin for a patient needing major surgery.

The next day Stephen died. Gloria was at his side sobbing, according to the nurses. I visited with Gloria at her house to plan the funeral service. Her husband was not there.

"Just have the standard committal service," she said.

She didn't seem too interested in making the service personal.

"Will there be other children at the service," I asked.

She didn't know.

"Who do you expect at the service?"

"The usual," she responded while she worked on knitting some baby booties.

"Are there any special scripture readings or poems or songs you want to include?"

"No," just the usual ones. "I trust your good judgment to provide the appropriate things."

The day of the committal service—she didn't want a church service or a ceremony at the funeral home—was a bright, spring day. It was odd that Gloria's husband still wasn't there. It was just me and Gloria.

"Is your husband coming?" I straight out asked Gloria that day.

"No, he doesn't do grief services. He's busy at work."

I just nodded and began the committal service.

Gloria, throughout the service, to comfort herself, was now knitting a baby's blanket.

The final prayer incorporated the sound of the birds, the fresh smell of the air, the wind caressing our faces as signs of God's renewal of the earth and promises that God would renew our spirits as well.

"Remind us that life goes on even in this place so that our faith might be strengthened and our hope renewed. This we ask in the name of the One who was once a child with a mother and whose love for us extends beyond this life and the grave. Amen."

I shook Gloria's hand and hugged her with my condolences. She said, "That's okay, Father, God will provide." She had a far away, disassociated look on her face.

The next week, while I was away, the State Department of Family Services had left a message on my answering machine regarding a recommendation for Gloria to adopt another child. They left a number to call to return the message. I didn't bother writing it down.

Chapter Nine

DO NOT FOLLOW THE BOUNCING BALL

He was dead ten years before we knew he was gone. "Thomas Sillman, July 6, 1993: Class of 1979" was all that was published in the necrology section of the alumni magazine. He would have found great irony, though, in the notice's setting between a story of a mission trip to Haiti and a request to give money to the Ivy league school.

"That's just like the church through the ages," he would have said. "Using the dead as an investment for the privileged with a few pennies thrown in to salve their consciences."

Thomas was more literate than I will ever be. He had not only read Flannery O'Connor, F. Scott Fitzgerald, Gide and Baudelaire, he could quote, using his prodigious memory, complete paragraphs from their works. The best I could do was the feeble response that I had heard of O'Conner and Fitzgerald and that I liked Camus' *The Plague.*

The old cliché that we came from vastly different worlds had more cachet here than in its usual applications.

He had invested in the life of his mind while I was busy working my way through school, just doing what I needed to get my homework done well enough to receive an "A." With the exception of one general survey course on American literature, I just didn't have much time or energy to read after finishing the shift at the plant, serving as student pastor of a very small church on the weekends and trying to find some time for my family.

That perhaps should have been something for me to reflect upon at the time. How did a man like Thomas—and it was always "Thomas" never "Tom"—have all that time? He was married to Carole and had two children, Marion and Sharon, ages five and seven. While it was also true that he served as student pastor of a small church while in college, it would not have been nearly enough income to provide even a rudimentary life for his family.

In fact, I was covetous of his self-indulgence in having the time and energy to ponder the greater issues of existence while I was out just trying to pay for the meager existence my family had. Condemning Thomas was beside the point for it was my own conscience that drove me to provide a middle class living for my family even at that cost of my own self-differentiation and deepening as a person.

It was difficult, although I do not think it had ever been attempted, to read great literature or classical philosophy while making direct clutches for a transmission at the Chevy plant. The foreman never said anything while I studied my notes for tests in the classes I was taking but it would be logistically impossible to read a book.

Wryly, it was often commented in the plant that a monkey and twelve bananas could do any one of our jobs because each was so mindlessly routine and unchallenging. But reading a book while making two thousand seven hundred fifty direct clutches every seven and ½ hours, was not something even the most advanced biped could do.

Thomas didn't have to worry about any of this while he was in undergraduate school. It was clear, from his appearance, he was his own person. He had thick blonde hair that reached his shoulders and a full beard of the same color. His eyes had a twinkle of mirth and wisdom in them that gave him added charisma when paired with his aristocratic Virginian accent.

Here, I hoped in my heart, was the kind of friend I never had time for in college. It was sixty miles, one way, from where I lived to the college and I always had to drive back to work. There was only time to drive to college, go to class and go home to work. Social aspects of the college life had to be forfeited entirely.

My hopes seemed to be validated at first for Thomas's family and mine would go to church together on Sunday, trying out the local churches and critiquing the sermons afterwards. We would share lunches after church and talk about the reviews in the New York Times Book Review.

Carole, with her long, straight brown hair and straightforward body posture got along well with my wife, Marilyn, canvassing everything from sewing to politics to childrearing. And, of course, my daughter, Michelle, could play with Marion and Sharon. This seemed like the ideal situation and it happened right at the beginning of our seminary experience. Was this some kind of affirmation that we were at the right place at the right time in our lives?

Thomas and Carole would often come over to our apartment in the married student housing section of the seminary. We would let our girls play together while we talked about religion and politics and art and literature. As I fell under the enchantment of his drawl and charisma, it occurred to me this must have been the same kind of accent Robert E. Lee or Thomas Jefferson had. This accent, and his grounding in literature, gave his pronouncements a greater weight at the wine and cheese parties we would host at our smallish, two bedroom student apartment.

People were enthralled b what he had to say because of the poetical pleasure induced as the words rolled off his tongue. When others, as home in the literature of the Western World as he was, would disagree with him in their dull Middle Atlantic or clipped Midwestern intonations, their statements were merely prosaic if not more often flat. Being such a close friend with Thomas and his family gave my life a reflected glory and made me, by association, look more learned than I was.

One night at our apartment, after the guests had consumed the cases of red and white wine we had purchased to benefit the Woman's Center, Thomas and Carole lingered after the other guests had left. It had become our custom to hold hands in a circle and pray together. The prayers covered the concerns of our seminary community, our lives and the world.

That night, after prayer, Thomas and Carole continued to hold our hands.

"Keith, you know you are my best friend," he began. I nodded but my wariness was suddenly activated.

"Last night," he went on, "I awoke in the middle of the night hugging my pillow and saying your name."

I was in shock. My palms were suddenly sweaty. I released his hand but still held tightly to Carole's. Marilyn was still holding Thomas' hand unaware of what was happening.

Thomas could tell from my facial gestures and my body language that this was not a pleasant thought to me. So, to sweeten the offer, I guess, he added, "If you go to bed with me, I will let you go to bed with Carole and I will bed Marilyn."

Here was an unexpected turn of events. A person who I wanted to love as a friend and brother wanted me for a kind of sexuality I was aware of but did not find palatable. The added incentive of sex with his wife just made the offer more despicable and Thomas a miscreant in my heart of hearts.

I mumbled some words, that I hoped were kind and nonjudgmental, about that not being my "thing." I hurried them out of the apartment.

"Are you sure that's what he was saying?" Marilyn asked.

Even though this was the first time I had ever been propositioned by a homosexual, I was certain of what it was. It puzzled me that Marilyn was not convinced. It was sweet of her to be more trusting in people and more willing to believe in their goodness than I was.

I know it seems a little more than ironic that my first encounter with a gay person who was interested in me was in seminary. So much for the idea that all the folks in divinity school were going to share my point of view or orientation. What a shock to find out what I had taken for friendship had been sexualized by the person I thought was going to help make-up for all the potential friendships I had foregone in college because of how much I had to work to put myself through.

We didn't socialize much with Thomas and Carole as a couple after that. They were still invited to our wine and cheese parties but we avoided being alone with them. In fact, Thomas's behavior over the next several months became a problem in the married student housing complex. He was more and more open about his sexual orientation and more progressively irresponsible about it.

Lovers from other cities would drop into his apartment and he would lock out his two little girls when they came home from school. The younger one, Marian, couldn't hold it any longer one day and actually wet her pants in the hallway outside her own apartment door. The married student government had to step in.

It wasn't long after that that Carole decided to leave Thomas. She said she was going back to Virginia to open a sewing shop. Carole and her daughters came over to our apartment for coffee and dessert and to say good-bye. I felt so sorry for them and so sad that what I had hoped would be a great relationship was ending in such pain. We gave her fifty dollars—in 1977 that was all we could afford from our own meager resources—and promised to stay in touch.

Thomas, however, was a more immediate problem. I saw him in class every day. His unwelcome proposition and daily presence gave me the occasion to reflect profoundly upon the nature of sexuality, grace and friendship. Did his desire for me indicate that I was gay and sending out signals to him of sexual attraction? Wasn't homosexuality denounced in the scriptures?

The fairly loose curriculum structure of the seminary offered me the opportunity to design my own class specifically on homosexuality and ponder these questions profoundly. I ordered every scholarly book I could put my hands on concerning homosexuality (this was in the days before the internet). The main library had an extensive collection of classical tomes that, without a dissenting murmur, denounced it: Augustine, Jerome, Luther, Calvin, et al.

But Masters and Johnsons had just published a new study that indicated not all homosexuals were alike. A significant percentage was pair bonded or desired to be pair bonded in a long term relationship. It sounded similar to relationships in the heterosexual community to me.

As for the scriptures, it was not hard to explain away or ignore the scriptural passages seemingly denouncing homosexuality. The references were either talking about homosexuality as an aberration in power dynamics or were so homophobic as to be hateful and, therefore, suspect as reflecting a loving god. One also can't get around the fact that people ignored scriptural pronouncements against women speaking in church ,killing, lying, etc. to serve their own convenience. It was clear to me that scripture was being used to assuage psychological concerns and assist in social cohesion by groups more interested in power than emotionally healthy relationships.

I concluded that my responsibility was to try and maintain contact with Thomas. The dangerous irresponsibility of his successive trysts with one lover after another indicated he was more deeply flawed than most of us. Condemning him or shunning him would not serve any healing purpose.

Besides, I said to myself, who said that loving your neighbor was easy? Didn't I aim to be more than just a routine believer? Didn't I want to be like the disciples risking the dangerous, attempting the difficult and defying the conventions of the bourgeois culture around me?

After a six month cooling off period of prayer and reflection, I decided to ask Thomas if he wanted to play tennis. We arranged for a time to meet at the courts near the married student housing complex.

It was a beautiful day. I had on a pair of tennis shorts I had purchased when I worked at the auto plant and had money. Thomas showed up in a pair of cut off blue jeans. We chatted and caught up on how his family was doing while we volleyed to warm up. It was a little awkward but it was what I felt I was called to do.

I turned my back on him to pick up the balls that were behind me on the court. When I bent over at the waist to pick them up, Thomas bellowed loudly, "Look at the great ass!"

I blushed and noted that I was fifty pounds overweight and had always thought of my ass as one of my least presentable parts. I quoted my mother saying, "If you've seen one crack, you've seen them all."

Thomas was shaking his head in disagreement and was ready to say something else unsavory when I hit the ball as hard as I could right at him. We continued a desultory game, in which I stayed out of conversational range, and then parted formally.

"It was really strange," I shared with Marilyn later than night. "That was the first time in my life that I have known what it was to be a person who is suffering the unwanted sexual attentions of someone else. This is what women go through all the time, isn't it?"

She nodded and coyly said, "Some don't consider it suffering. " We made love that night to "Scheherazade" by Rimsky-Korsakov.

Thomas and I never met socially again.

Thirty years have passed since then. I do not know what the quality of his life was in that time. It saddens me to think about how he was so disconnected from his classmates his death notice was barer than dry bones. Ten years gone before anyone knew. Thomas Sillman, like all God's wayward children, deserved more than that.

Chapter Ten

MARY HAD A BABY—TYRICE?

The inner city church choir warbled out the old
Christmas spiritual:

Mary had a baby, oh, Lord,

Mary had a baby, oh my Lord,

Mary had a baby, oh Lord,

People keep a-coming' an' the train done gone.

What did she name him? oh, Lord,

What did she name him? oh my Lord,

What did she name him? oh Lord,

People keep a-comin' an' the train done gone.

She named him Jesus, oh, Lord,

She named him Jesus, oh my Lord,

She named him Jesus, oh Lord,

People keep a-comin' an' the train done gone.

No one in the pews bothered to clap along except
Mary. She wasn't the only Mary in the congregation. She
wasn't even the only pregnant Mary in the church that
Sunday morning. But she was the only black woman named
Mary who was pregnant with an Italian man's baby
"without benefit of clergy" as used to be said in more
genteel times.

That made her an outcast in the black community as well as the Italian community. She may have been without a Joseph and she didn't have a car, let alone a donkey to ride, but she had no place to stay just as the story goes about that Mary at Bethlehem so long ago.

I had been working hard that year to try to convince Planned Parenthood and Birthrite, a right to life organization, to communicate and work together on that which they could agree. They had sent representatives to the church I was working with for a conference on abortion and women's health. Fools rush in where angels fear to tread.

"Abortion is feticide. Killing is against the Bible."

"The death of a fetus in the Old Testament does not incur the same punishment as the death of a human being."

"The overall thrust of the Bible is to protect the weak against the machinations of the powerful."

"In that case, it is men, in positions of power, who tell women what to do with their embryos and fetuses. When the conceived being in the womb has no viable existence of its own, it is part of the woman's body and that is a matter for the woman to decide not powerful men."

"Planned Parenthood was founded by a woman, not a man."

"Exactly, women began then to take responsibility for their own health and their own bodies."

"We are an organization almost completely of women who helps other women who decide to keep their child rather than have an abortion. You would not believe the number of young women who need a place to stay to give birth to their child."

"It is wonderful that women have that choice. But it is their choice even in the way you describe the child as "their child.""

"Wouldn't it be a way to empower women," I chimed in, "to expand the opportunities for those who choose to bring the fetus/embryo to term to have a place to do so?"

I was surprised that they both agreed. Perhaps they were just being polite since I was pastor, okay student pastor, of the host church. That was when the idea was born in me to look into creating a facility for women who needed a place to stay if circumstances made them homeless and/or alienated from their family.

Another journey into realms angels are smart enough to have abandoned some time ago. No organization—on either the prochoice or the prolife side—wanted to fund a study of what such a facility would look like. I drove back and forth over the Fairhaven Bridge going from organization to organization sharing the idea and looking for financial support.

Waiting in my car for the bridge to turn back to its home position so auto traffic could roll, the solution came to me. There were governmental rumblings about replacing the Fairhaven Bridge. It was ninety years old, expensive to maintain and an inconvenient, anachronistic way to manage boat traffic on the Quinnipiac River. But to the people of the neighborhood, it was more than just a part of the scenery: they identified with it. It was like them: hardworking, gritty, a little passed over by the times.

The rallying cry had gone out, "Save the bridge." T-shirts with a picture of the bridge had been made and sold. So, why not commemorative plates? It seems stodgy in today's light but people still buy commemorative plates of all kinds of things. Royal weddings come to mind.

We found a manufacturer of commemorative plates and arranged to have one thousand made; I fronted the money to pay the cost. If we sold every plate, we would have a $10,000 profit to use to fund a study of a facility with a program to assist women who had chosen to bring their babies to term but had no place to stay.

The money was raised. A pediatrician, working on her Masters of Public Health at Yale, was hired to do a research study and create a proposal for a facility and program. She helped us develop a program for fifteen to nineteen year old women who needed a place to stay in order to give birth. The day care part of the facility would provide a source of employment for the girls and women and child care for the mother's children while the members of the program continued their education. It would also provide some of the monies needed to fund the program as the day care would be open to paying members of the community. We called it S.H.I.P.-- Shelter Home for Infants and Parents.

S.H.I.P. would have been very helpful for my mother who dropped out of high school and gave birth to me when she was seventeen years old. If she had a place that would have provided child care, flexible hours of employment, social support, counseling and parental education, her life would have been much easier. So, yes, this program would have filled not only a community need, but a personal one as well.

My keen personal interest in this might have been what David Arnold, a professor in the pastoral counseling department at Yale, picked up on when I asked for his help.

He was said to have a particular interest in family and children concerns so I was hoping he would lend his name and credibility to S.H.I.P.

"Do you know anyone who would be willing to throw his or her personal support and prestige behind something such as this?" I was leaning toward Professor Arnold.

He sat back in his chair and noncommittally said, "Not off hand." He began picking his nose right in front of me! That was not only not the answer I was hoping for, sticking his finger up his nose seemed weird.

He was a counseling professor, right? He didn't just pick his nose because he had a booger that was bothering him. Was there something else he was trying to communicate to me? Was the intensity of my interest a red flag to him?

Did I have a big booger hanging out of my nose? Was I putting his nose out of joint by putting him on the spot? Was he telling me to keep my own nose clean before being concerned about anyone else's nose? Was it a way of saying he had his own issues to be concerned about? Was it a way of lowering his prestige in my eyes so I would not make any further effort to solicit his help? Or, to borrow from Freud, was this one of those times when a booger was just a booger?

If he wanted me to leave him alone, it worked. I never approached him again and we averted gazes when passing in the hallways at the seminary. But I still have not developed the same sophisticated—if you call public nose picking sophisticated—way of putting others off.

That modern day Mary, clapping along to the Christmas spiritual that day in worship, was the reason I had been approached by Birthrite in the first place. She had no place to stay, they said. Her own family had disowned her and the father of the baby could have nothing to do with her lest his own family disown him. Marriage was out of the question in those days before improving race relations made multiracial relationships more common.

"Do you have someone in your congregation who could help her out?" they asked me.

"No," I responded, "but we might be able to work something out."

Bless my wife, Marilyn's heart. She had no objections to allowing a homeless, pregnant, black woman bereft of family to move in. The organization would pay for her groceries and provide transportation to doctor's appointments. Our only commitment would be to give her space in the old Queen Victorian parsonage we lived in.

"After all," the queen of the manse quickly said, "we have plenty of room in this old place. What could it hurt and it might even help someone without costing us anything."

"There is only one thing," she said, "no smoking in our house. Michelle has enough problems with allergies and asthma without having to deal with cigarette smoke."

"We'll make that clear to her when she moves in."

And we did. But this Mary, unlike the Biblical one, I presume, was an avid smoker. I would come home from Wednesday night choir practices and see a plume of smoke coming out of her bedroom window. Mary thought if she blew the smoke out of the window we would be none the wiser. We could smell the smoke on her, though, and continually asked her to stop for the sake of her baby. Smoking must also affect one's hearing as well, for she didn't stop—not even the first time I drove her to the hospital to have the baby.

Mary had her car window down the entire way to the hospital puffing on her fag. She even stopped before entering the hospital to finish her cig.

That turned out to be a practice run. False labor contractions.

Since Mary was such a chain smoker and wouldn't abide by our house rules, we redoubled our efforts to find her an apartment that had subsidized rent. We did not want her living with us when the baby came. She may have decided to keep the baby but we were committed to not keep Mary. We needed her to live in her own place where she could smoke to her heart's content. It may not have been good for the baby, but there is only so much one can do for another person.

I did what I could to quickly refurbish the apartment one of the parishioners had given for her use. Paneling was put on the wall. The window wells and woodwork were painted and new carpeting was installed. It wasn't the Ritz but it wasn't a manger either.

We saw to it that there were no animals in this modern stable, either. The exterminator had taken care of that. Camels, donkeys and cows are hard to find in urban settings and cockroaches are eager to take their places.

The second trip to the hospital with Mary experiencing labor pains turned out to be the real thing. I accompanied her to the maternity ward and settled into the maternity waiting room. "Rudolph the Red Nosed

Reindeer" was on the television. Rudolph hadn't even been asked, yet, to guide the sleigh when the delivery nurse came out with the good news.

"Congratulations! You are the father of a new baby boy!"

My face reddened. "I am not really the father. I am just a friend who brought her over."

The nurse gave me such a condemnatory smirk that I knew that she had heard that before from white men who brought in black women to have cream colored babies!

This modern Mary's story turned out just like the Biblical Mary's that is commemorated in the song: she had a baby. That she named him Tyrice does not rob this Christmas story of its poignancy or relevance for our responsibility to welcome the stranger, provide shelter for the homeless and clothe the naked.

There may not have been angels hosannaing when Mary laid Tyrice in his new cradle but we raised our own chorus of hallelujahs because she no longer lived with us. Those long ago angels could have not been happier, nor sung with more fervor, than we did.

www.ingramcontent.com/pod-product-compliance
Lightning Source LLC
Chambersburg PA
CBHW072022060426

42449CB00033B/1603